DIARY OF A JOURNEY ACROSS TIBET

DIARY
OF
A JOURNEY ACROSS TIBET

BY

HAMILTON BOWER

GYAN

ISBN : 978-81-212-1535-0(HB)

First Published, 1893

Published, 2018

Published by

Gyan Publishing House
5, Ansari Road
Daryaganj, New Delhi-110002
Phone: 011-47034999, 9811692060
www.gyanbooks.com
E-mail: books@gyanbooks.com

Printed at: G. Print Process, Delhi.

MASKED MONKS AT HEMIS.

THIS RECORD OF

A JOURNEY ACROSS TIBET

IS BY PERMISSION DEDICATED TO

HIS EXCELLENCY

THE MOST NOBLE THE MARQUIS OF LANSDOWNE

G.C.S.I., G.C.M.G., G.C.I.E.

LATE VICEROY AND GOVERNOR-GENERAL OF INDIA

THROUGH WHOSE SUPPORT AND PATRONAGE THE PROJECT

WAS CARRIED OUT

BY HIS OBLIGED AND HUMBLE SERVANT

THE AUTHOR

PREFACE

THIS book is the plain unvarnished diary kept during my journey across Tibet and China, written often with half-frozen fingers in a tent on the Chang, or by a flickering light in Chinese rest-houses, a chapter on the Country, Religion, Fauna, etc., only having since been added. Under these circumstances I hardly feel it necessary to assure my readers that the book lays no claim to literary merit or style. At one time I thought of endeavouring to evolve something of a form likely to be more popular, but abstained, fearing that should I succeed in doing so it would only be at the cost of diminishing its value to those interested in geographical research, and to those who may be contemplating travel in the same or similar regions. Those are the people for whom this volume is primarily intended, and the author's highest aim is to convey a faithful impression of travel in Tibet.

I would draw the attention of those wishing to get an idea of the marvellous physical configuration of the Chang, or great Tibetan plateau, to the sectional plan at the end of the volume. This Chang is by far the highest and largest plateau on the face of the earth,—compared to it the Pamirs, the so-called Roof of the World, sink into insignificance. An interesting feature of the country explored was the large salt lakes met with at elevations often much greater than that of the summit of Mont Blanc.

To my companion, Surgeon-Captain W. G. Thorold, I.M.S., whose love of travel caused him to make considerable sacrifices to accompany me, my thanks are due for much assistance. In times of danger and difficulty I always felt that I had in him a staunch companion and sound adviser.

The map is principally the work of Sub-surveyor Atma Ram, who paced every yard of the way from where we crossed the Kashmir frontier till we embarked on a tributary of the Yang-tse. This work was checked by my own astronomical observations. The altitudes were taken by hypsometer and aneroid. Captain O. B. S. Shore, 18th Bengal Lancers, has, with the assistance of some indifferent photographs done by myself with a hand camera, drawn the greater part of the illustrations, for which my thanks are due to him, as also to Mr. C. V. Hunter and Mr. W. Woodville Rockhill for some excellent photographs. My acknowledgments are also due to Mr. H. Seebohm, F.L.S., F.Z.S., for kindly supplying valuable notes on Birds in the last chapter (XVI.) of the book.

The spelling of proper names is as nearly phonetic as possible with languages having such different sounds as Tibetan and English.

UNITED SERVICE CLUB,
SIMLA, 1894.

CONTENTS

LIST OF ILLUSTRATIONS

CHAPTER I

FROM SIMLA TO THE FRONTIER

On my return from Turkistan in 1890, after an absence of fourteen months, thoroughly bitten with the love of travel that seems to come to everybody who has once experienced the charm of wandering amongst the peaks, passes, and glaciers of the Himalayas, I began to turn my thoughts towards the mysterious land of Tibet.

In Ladakh I had already become acquainted with a people almost identically the same as the subjects of Lhasa, with the same monasteries, Lamas, and praying-wheels; and perpetually muttering the same eternal reiteration of *Om mani padmi hum* ("Oh, the flowers in the lotus leaf, oh!"). But away to the east lay the true Tibet, a huge white blank on our maps; and that blank I determined to visit. On the southern part a few names of places and routes visited by native explorers were marked, but of the centre and north we knew as little as if it had been in another planet. The first thing was to find out whether the Government of India would be inclined to look favourably on the scheme, but my doubts on that point were quickly set at rest. His Excellency the Viceroy not only sanctioned the idea but gave assistance in forwarding the project, and through the kindness of Lord Roberts, a companion, Dr. W. G. Thorold of the Indian Medical Service, was allowed to accompany me.

The instruments I decided to take were :—Maximum and minimum thermometers; a 3-inch explorer's theodolite, by Cooke; three ordinary thermometers to register low temperatures; hypsometer, by Hicks, with several spare thermometers; bull's-eye lantern; three prismatic compasses; a pocket chronometer; a micrometer; several pocket compasses, and three aneroids. These, with sheets of drying paper between wire frames, and arsenical soap, to hold botanical and for natural history specimens respectively, made up the scientific equipment of the expedition.

As regards medicines we took an Army Railway Medical Companion, to which were added a few medicines for diseases of the eye, vaseline, and iodoform; vaseline is an absolute essential, as on the plateaux of Central Asia, owing to the high winds and extreme dryness, the skin of the hands and face gets terribly chapped, while mixed with iodoform it makes an absolutely perfect dressing for horses' sore backs. I would advise future travellers in those regions to take some paregoric as well, as colds and coughs have to be guarded against.

For clothing we equipped ourselves in thick puttoo, a sort of native woollen cloth made in Kashmir, with warm woollen underclothing, and sheep-skin robes. Our boots were the ordinary infantry ammunition pattern, made a good deal too large, so as to be able to wear several pairs of thick woollen socks; the latter were all made of double thickness at the toes and heels. A dozen chamois leather skins for patching clothes were also taken.

For bedding we had felts, lamb-skin rugs, and blankets; blankets alone are of little use against great cold, and no amount of woollen clothes will keep out the wind on the Chang (Central Tibetan plateau), so skins must be taken.

Our battery consisted of two double-barrelled ·500 express rifles, one 12-bore shot gun, two cavalry regulation carbines, and three revolvers. We had about 300 rounds for the express rifles, 200 for the shot gun, mostly No. 6; 200 for the carbines, and one or two packets of revolver ammunition.

Dr. Thorold and myself rode on troopers' saddles. These have great advantages over ordinary hunting saddles; in the first place a carbine can be carried in the bucket, and so is always handy for defence. The chances are that it may never be required for that purpose; but if it is required, it is required very badly, and if carried anywhere else is almost certain not to be handy at the right moment. Besides, when riding along, should a chance of shooting an antelope occur, as continually happens at the most unexpected moments, one has it handy. Moreover, a trooper's saddle will easily carry a greatcoat, lunch, field glasses, etc.

It is absolutely necessary to have some literature, on these sorts of expeditions, as the mind yearns for food. Books being heavy and transport limited, nothing that will not bear re-reading should be taken. Our library consisted of Shakespeare, Napier's *Peninsular War* and Carlyle's *Sartor Resartus.* Books, instruments, and clothes were all stowed in Kashmir-made leather-bound *yak dans*, two of which formed General Kinloch's *pattern bed* and were long enough to hold gun barrels. Our tents consisted of a sepoy's *pal* (a tent with the roof sloping down to the ground and no side walls), 10 feet long and 6 feet high, one slightly longer for the caravan drivers, the inside of an 80-lb. Kabul tent and a *tente d'abri* to serve as kitchen; all were of cotton, and except the last they were lined with puttoo, but I am inclined to think that an extra cotton lining would be a more effectual protection against the wind.

On the 4th April 1891 I left Simla, and having paid a flying visit to my regiment *en route*, arrived at Srinagar on the 16th. At Murree the snow lay deep, and the road for the first stage or two was in a very bad state; in one place the tonga capsized, very nearly sending all hands over the cliff; however, we picked ourselves up and soon were under weigh again, none the worse.

At Srinagar, where I was in a few days joined by Dr. Thorold, my time was taken up buying transport animals, fitting pack saddles, etc. Starting into an unknown country, it is very difficult to decide what animals are the best for the work. Yaks have the great advantage of being insensible to high altitudes; in fact they cannot live at low ones, and in Western Tibet are practically never seen below about 12,000 feet. They stand cold better than any other animal, but their use is precluded by the many serious faults they possess. They won't eat grain, therefore it is impossible to get them over an absolutely barren stretch that takes more than four or five days to cross. They also march very slowly, and if the ground is stony soon get footsore.

Ponies, relieved by yaks when crossing difficult passes, are largely used in the trade between India and Turkistan. Several breeds are employed, foremost amongst which comes in point of numbers the pony known in India as the Yarkandi, though the name is misapplied, as in Yarkand no pony or horse raising is done, the little land available being cultivated like a garden, and much too valuable to be used as grazing ground. The ponies brought down from those parts are mostly raised by the Kirghiz on the Pamirs and steppes. They are strong hardy brutes, well able to stand cold, and can carry a load of 250 lbs.; but my experience has been that when grass is scarce and grain runs out, the so-called Yarkandi knocks up sooner than some of the smaller breeds. In appearance he is coarse and heavy-looking, standing about thirteen hands, with a thick mane and tail, stout limbs, and dull eye, often ewe-necked. Greys predominate, but not to the same extent as amongst Kabulis, a breed to which they seem to bear cousinship. Many of the Cossacks ride ponies of a similar kind. In Kashgar I have seen a stamp of pony very similar, but with the ewe-neck more pronounced; they are called Kazaks and come from the Russian steppes. I was told that they were very impatient of heat, and one that was in my possession seemed much distressed when the weather got warm, and was continually bleeding from the small veins on the shoulder. My caravanbashi assured me that it was the sign of a good one to work, and certainly that pony was a marvel in the amount of work he could do on short rations.

The Ladakh ponies, thick-set little fellows about eleven hands high, are excellent workers, but are always in such poor condition in spring and early summer that one cannot reckon on getting more than a stray one here and there fit to start on a journey. The Kashmir ponies, very small and slight, are well-plucked; they must be got from some of the remote valleys, not from the marshy lands about the capital. But mules beat ponies, and the only difficulty is to get enough of them, and of the right class. The Hindustani mule is not suitable; those brought to Ladakh from the country about Lhasa, short and thick-set, are *par excellence* the animals for work in a cold mountainous country.

My original idea was to have put all clothes, instruments, etc., on ponies or mules and to have used sheep to carry supplies. A sheep can carry 30 lbs. easily, can pick up a living on very scanty grass, and with a bag of flour on his back he presents a perambulating meal complete. Unfortunately, however, the winter had been a very severe one. Great losses had occurred amongst the flocks, and sheep in sufficiently good condition to start on a journey were not procurable, so the caravan had to be made up of ponies, donkeys, and mules. My pack saddles were the kind used on the Turkistan road, made out of a sort of reed that grows in the swamps about Yarkand; its advantages are lightness, the protection it gives from cold, suppleness (a horse can roll without breaking it), and if it sustains damage it can be mended by any caravan driver; the disadvantage is, that it is perhaps slightly more liable to give sore backs than saddles of European pattern.

On the 17th April 1891, accompanied by Mr. E. F. Knight, author of *Where Three Empires Meet*, *The Cruise of the Falcon*, etc., I left Srinagar. Dr. Thorold had already gone on to Leh. From Gunderbal, which is reached by water, the road runs up the beautiful Sind valley to the Zoji La Pass; though this pass is very low, being only 11,300 feet high, yet, owing to the amount of the snow that falls early in the season, it is often difficult to cross, and this year (1891) it was unusually so. The only way to get our things over was to have them made into very light packages and carried by coolies, while to each pony a man was told off to help him through the deep snow; it was a long weary day, and we were very glad when the small village of Matiyan, an island amidst a waste of snow, appeared in sight. Four marches further on Mānés[1] and Chortens[2] appeared; and the people being of a Mongolian type, we began to feel ourselves in a Buddhist country. Leh was reached on the 1st of June, and I halted there for thirteen days making final preparations. The difficulty about enlisting men was increased by my refusal to say what was the object of the expedition. Numbers of Tibetans from beyond the frontier were in the bazaar, and had it leaked out that we were going to their country, on crossing the frontier we should probably have met a party ready to oppose our progress. However, six men willing to go and to ask no questions were enlisted through the assistance kindly rendered by the Naib Wazir (assistant or lieutenant-governor). These men, with the exception of one, who however was far and away the most intelligent of the lot, bore

[1] Heaps of stones on which are carved mystical sacred sentences common all over Tibet.

[2] Monuments.

MONKS ARRAYED FOR A MASKED DANCE.

Though there are habitations farther on, there is no cultivation, and consequently very little except mutton is procurable. From Tankse I hired some yaks and ponies, wishing to spare our own animals as much as possible, and having halted for one day we continued our route towards Chang Chenmo. The first march was to Chakka Talao, up the bed of a stream containing numbers of small trout-like fish. On the road, at an elevation of fully 14,000 feet, I saw numbers of locusts; and Dr. Thorold, who ascended the hills in search of game, reported having seen some at 16,000 feet. The hills present the mosaic-like appearance common in Ladakh—sharply defined patches of yellow and dark brown.

When we got into camp I had quite an argument with the caravan drivers, who follow the iniquitous practice that exists on the Yarkand road, of tying up the ponies after getting into camp. After a march of nine or ten hours they tie them up so as to prevent them grazing for two hours or more, and then give them a feed of barley, after which they are turned loose. The consequence is that their stomachs, being empty and weakened by the long fast, fail to digest the grain. Besides, when grass is scanty, as it is in all these countries, cutting two hours off their grazing time is a serious matter, and instead of resting, the poor animals wander about the whole night hunting for whatever they can pick up. When I gave the order that they were to be turned loose directly we halted, the caravan drivers with horror-stricken faces protested, saying that such an outrage against "Dustoor" (custom), the god of India, would assuredly lead to our being left without any transport in a few days. I persisted, however, and had I not done so, we should never have got across Tibet.

Our next march was to Pobrang, which consists of a few huts with grass close by, surrounded by barren hills. On the road, the west end of the Pangong Lakes is passed; they are salt, contain no fish, though plenty are found in the rivers flowing in, and are of a beautiful deep blue colour. We bought a Tibetan sheep-dog here, to guard the camp, for four rupees. These dogs are something like big powerfully built collies, and are excellent as watch dogs; but one never gets fond of them, as they possess nothing of the nobleness of character that European dogs have, and are generally of a suspicious and cowardly nature.

Next day we moved to Langkar Mo, altitude 16,600 feet, close to the Marsamik La, or Langkar La pass, as the natives more generally call it. There is a small dilapidated shelter here, but as it was snowing, we decided that our tents would be a more effectual protection. Numbers of kiang (*Equus hemionus*), the Tibetan wild ass, an animal exceedingly common all over these high tablelands, were seen on the road. The Marsamik La is a very easy pass, even as we found it, with a considerable amount of snow lying on the north side; and the ponies were easily got over, but one of our men was quite

PANGONG LAKE FROZEN OVER IN APRIL.

knocked up with mountain sickness. We saw some female *Ovis ammon* grazing on a hill-side.

At Pamzal, 29th June; 15,475 feet.—In the Chang Chenmo valley, the depôt of supplies I had sent on was awaiting us. It consisted of thirty-three maunds[1] of chopped straw, four maunds of suttoo, five maunds of flour, six maunds of rice, and a hundred sets of horse-shoes. Suttoo, called tsampa farther east, is made from barley, which is first put into boiling water, then parched over a fire, and afterwards ground. Being already partially cooked, it has the great advantage over flour that it can be eaten without additional cooking by adding a little water—a great consideration where fuel is scarce and sometimes unprocurable. After leaving Pamzal, some of our own ponies had to be loaded, much against my inclination; but, owing to the backwardness of the season, the hired animals were in very poor condition, and kept breaking down.

The man who previously told me he had gone to Polu with Carey and Dalgleish had been lying all the time, not having even the faintest idea where the pass is. A Ladakhi, however, who had come with the hired animals, acknowledged that he had been across the frontier to a place five marches distant to get salt, and on being promised a reward offered to show the road; under his direction we pursued our way towards the Lanak La, crossing two small easy passes *en route*. A couple of hired yaks died on the

[1] Maund = 82 lbs.

way, and we had considerable difficulty in getting the others along, our things not arriving one evening until after dark. Antelopes were to be seen, and I shot five Tibetan sand-grouse;[1] they were absurdly tame, simply waddling away as the caravan passed; four were shot on the ground with one barrel and another with the other barrel as they flew off.

The Kashmiri who had been knocked up from mountain sickness on the Marsamik La did not seem to be getting any better, so before crossing the Lanak La he was sent back. He was one of those men quite unable to live at great altitudes.

[1] See page 294.

CHAPTER II

COMMENCEMENT OF EXPLORATION

3rd July 1891.—Crossed the frontier at the Lanak La, and after marching 24 miles, which took us nine hours, camped. The pass is easy, and there was no snow on it.

Tobomarpo, 4th July; 15 miles, 17,550 feet.—Down a nullah all the way to camp, where there is water, grass, and fuel. Just after starting, a donkey knocked up; the men with the hired transport, who had been dismissed at the last camp, not being out of hail, we called to them that they could have the donkey, and I have not the slightest doubt that they got it back to Tankse alive. A messenger arrived with news from the Resident at Kashmir, saying that the rumour of Mr. Lennard's murder was unfounded. [Minimum Temperature, 17° Fahrenheit.[1]]

Kalung, 5th July; 18 miles, 17,680 feet.—South of a small lake. Easy marching all the way. Grass seems much more plentiful this side than it is within

[1] For Minimum Temperature at each halting-place, see Chart, page 302 *sqq.*

our frontier. A strong west wind was blowing all day; this wind, which sometimes had a good deal of south in it, accompanied us all the way across Tibet, and always seemed to get stronger in the afternoon; the warmest time of the day being the morning before 9 A.M. Boortsa (*Eurotia*), the staple fuel in Ladakh and on the Turkistan road, was still plentiful, but farther on it failed us, and the only fuel procurable was argols.[1]

6th July, Papuk; 17,694 feet.—After leaving the small lake lying to the north of our last camp, we approached the Mangtza Cho Lake, and camped to the south of it. It is a fine sheet of water, of a deep indigo-blue, at an elevation of 16,540 feet. Round the lake there is an incrustation of salt, and people from Ladakh and Noh come for it in summer. South of the lake there is a fine snowy peak, and to the north-west another. As grass was plentiful I decided to halt for a day, in order to give the ponies a good feed and a rest. The sky was very much obscured by clouds (cumulo-cirrus and strato-cirrus), and I failed to get an observation for latitude. The Ladakhi guide said that from the east end of the lake there are three roads—one to the north followed by Messrs. Carey and Dalgleish, going to Polu, one towards the south going to Noh, and one going eastward that he had never traversed; but he had heard that at a place, five marches distant, Khamba nomads are often met with. He wanted to go back, but suspecting

[1] The droppings of wild yak.

his ignorance to be only feigned (owing to fear of the Tibetans), I decided to take him on *nolens volens*, as he had originally agreed to go five marches farther. There were a great number of wild yak tracks about the camp, but we did not see any of the animals themselves. At this time of year they probably are not usually hereabouts.

8th July, Camp 1; 13 miles, 17,650 feet (by aneroid).—Our guide, in accordance with his professions of ignorance of the road, was unable to give any name for this place; and all camps after this point will have to be known by numbers only. Khamba, according to his latest statement, was not 5 but 45 marches distant—a pretty considerable difference, and much more likely to be true. The signs of wild yak increased, and two were found lying dead in a nullah close to the camp. This is said to be a favourite hunting ground of the Rudok men, who come here to graze their flocks. Fortunately we met none of them, as had we done so, difficulties might have arisen.

9th July, Camp 2; 16 miles, 17,850 feet.—Leaving the lake behind, and passing some hot springs where there were flowers in bloom, we held due east and crossed a very easy pass, 18,025 feet high. A snowy range seemed to block the road, and I was much exercised in my mind as to how we were to cross it. The guide, though still sticking to his original statement that he had never been in these parts, said that the range could be crossed towards the southern end.

Away to the north of us magnificent snowfields were to be seen.

One of the caravan drivers was suffering much from his eyes, and our only bandage having been requisitioned for a pony that had been kicked, a shirt had to be torn into strips as a substitute.

10th July, Camp 3; 20 miles, 17,935 feet.—We crossed a pass, and then going south of a small lake, crossed another, 18,400 feet high, and came down on a very long lake running roughly north and south at a height of 17,930 feet, with several islands on it, the highest lake in Tibet and probably the highest in the world. To the south a snow-clad range, and on the other sides undulating hills, which towards the north appeared very barren, were to be seen. The Ladakhi guide appeared to have a great dread of the Khamba people, and did nothing but tell wonderful stories about them. When I remarked that he must have been in their country to have such an accurate knowledge of their habits, he utterly denied it, professing total ignorance as to what country we are in or where we are likely to get to.

11th July, Camp 4; 15 miles, 17,990 feet.—Just after leaving camp we sighted our first yak—a fine big bull grazing close to the water edge. Dr. Thorold went after him, and getting within easy distance, opened fire, hitting him five or six times before he fell, and though after he was wounded he had his assailant full in view, he made no attempt to charge. A buffalo or bison under the same circumstances

TIBETAN NOMADS.

would most assuredly have shown fight. Numbers of Tibetan antelope were to be seen in every direction.

On this march we managed to get into a *cul de sac* and had to cast back. A beautiful high snowy peak was seen far away to the north. From the snowy peaks on the south a fairly large stream flows into the lake which at that end is not so clear and much less salt than at the other. Gulls, bar-headed geese,[1] and divers were feeding at the mouth, and the omnipresent croaking Brahminy duck (*Casarca rutila*) flapped lazily over our heads, bold in the strength of his inferiority as a bird for the *cuisine.*

12th July, Camp 5; 16 miles, 18,315 feet.—We started in light variable winds, a change from the strong westerly wind we had been accustomed to, and a very pleasant one. When the wind calms down, life at these altitudes is quite pleasant, but when the typical west wind of the Chang is blowing, one's thoughts fly back to countries where people live in houses and have fires to warm themselves by. Some of the going was very bad quicksand-like soil, in which the ponies and mules sank up to the hocks and the donkeys had to be unladen, their loads being carried across on men's backs. Yaks appeared to be getting more plentiful: we saw three herds, one of twenty-one, one of seven, and one of six; but having abundance of meat in camp we did not shoot any. There was great excitement in the caravan owing to the appearance of what was taken to be a man in the

[1] See page 300.

distance, but on getting a field-glass to bear on it, it turned out to be a kiang facing us.

The Ladakhi guide complained of his eyes, and said they were so bad that he could not go on, but Dr. Thorold, after examination, pronounced that he had been malingering by tampering with them, so his discharge was deferred. Crossed an easy pass of 18,590 feet, but every one felt the effects of the high altitude. At the place we camped there was very little grass, so a ration of chopped straw was served out to all the animals. Sky nearly obscured all day by cirrus and strato-cirrus clouds.

13th July, Camp 6; 22 miles, 17,815 feet.—Straight up a broad valley with a good deal of ground of a quicksand nature, and then by a gradual ascent and descent over a pass 18,550 feet. On the road Thorold got a shot at a goa (Tibetan gazelle) and broke its leg. Our Tibetan dog started in pursuit, but with only three legs the goa went straight away from the dog with the greatest of ease. An antelope was bagged shortly afterwards: with so much game about, we had to manage to shoot something every day in order to economise supplies, and as a rule we had little difficulty in doing so. In the afternoon I rode on ahead looking for grass and water; a sudden turn in the valley disclosed to view a large lake straight in front, and in a small side nullah the requisite necessaries, grass, water, and fuel, were found. Grass being particularly plentiful, we decided to halt for a day, as the ponies badly required a rest.

Next morning I started for the lake with the necessary instruments to take the altitude. From the camp it appeared to be three miles off, but I found that the clear dry atmosphere had deceived me, and it was really about nine miles. As I came back a number of kiang kept circling round me, forming line and wheeling like a troop of cavalry. Little bird life was to be seen, some ravens and a few little brown birds being the only representatives of feathered nature. Though a halt, we did not spend it in idleness, all hands being kept busy shoeing ponies and washing clothes. I tried hard to get an observation for latitude, but the sky was much obscured by clouds (cumulo-cirrus and strato-cirrus), and towards evening a gale of wind sprang up that made it impossible to do anything. We battened our tents well down with stones, and spent a restless night expecting them to be carried away every minute; that they stood at all was a mystery to me.

15th July, Camp 7; 25 miles, 16,189 feet.—A very long march across a pass and with no water on the road. Towards evening the animals felt the want of it very much, and kept rushing into every watercourse only to find that they were all dry. The Ladakhi guide said the only water he knew of was the lake, which was less salt at this end than the other. I begged leave to doubt its being drinkable, but as darkness was setting in, and wandering on indefinitely in the dark was not to be thought of, we went towards the lake, picking our way over crusted salt and mud. We reached the edge only to find it as salt as the sea. Then we tried digging a few yards from the edge, and got some water, a trifle less salt, but of no use as a quencher of thirst. However, there was nothing to do but halt till daybreak. No grass and great difficulty in collecting a little fuel. At night, being very thirsty, I asked the Ladakhi when we would find water, and was told, "if it is the will of God, we will find it to-morrow." Towards morning a hailstorm set in, and filling the kettle with hailstones we soon were enjoying a cup of tea, and, much refreshed, resumed our march.

16th July, Camp 8; 16 miles, 16,500 feet.—After leaving the last camp we marched along the shores of the lake, and near the south-east corner found a magnificent spring of clear water discharging an enormous volume into the lake: the animals simply rushed into it.

A river of a dirty red colour flows into the east end, but requires some looking for, having high steep banks that completely conceal it from the view of any one a little distance off. While we were pitching camp a black spot on the opposite side of the valley was seen, which, on being examined with a field-glass, was made out to be a nomad's tent. A further search disclosed to view some sheep grazing on a hill close by, so I sent men over to make inquiries, telling them to describe us as merchants *en route* to China. They came back, bringing some milk and reporting there were no men at the tents, but five women, who said that in five days we should reach the head-quarters of the Khamba people, and that there were tents to be met with all the way.

17th July, Camp 9; 5 miles, 16,899 feet.—We crossed the river—a very difficult operation, as the bottom was of treacherous quicksand-like nature, and halted near the nomads' camp, which is called Gongma. Found a lot of geese, too young to fly, on a pool of water; they were excellent in the pot. As we approached the Khambas' tents, two men with long matchlocks with a two-pronged rest on the end approached. On each side of their faces their hair hung down in locks, and they seemed taller and slighter than typical Tibetans. In their belts, stuck diagonally across the body in front, they had straight swords, with scabbards ornamented with silver incrustations and turquoises, and in their hands they carried long spears. Their garments consisted of sheepskin robes of a very dirty colour with the hair inside, which were held up at the waist by a belt in such a manner that, while the upper part was very full, the lower did not reach to the knees—thus giving it a very kilt-like appearance. Their knees were bare, and on their feet they wore bright-coloured stockings, made of thick woollen cloth, soled with yak's skin and coming well up the calf, where they were tied with tape. They are true nomads, living in small black tents, which they move about to different places according to the season of the year, sowing no crops, and dependent for an existence on their herds of sheep, yaks, and horses. We had a long *Pow-wow* with them. They were very inquisitive as to who we were, and they could not make out where we were going, as they said the Lhasa road lay to the south, and the Yarkand to the north; I answered that we were merchants going to China, and had lost our way in the mountains. They said that in a south-westerly direction lay Khamba, which was thickly inhabited by nomads, but they absolutely refused to take us there, saying that the people would gather to oppose us, and they would certainly have their throats cut for bringing strangers into the country. But they offered to guide us for four days in a southerly direction to a place where there were four tents, and from there we could reach Sakhi on the Leh-Lhasa road in two. They utterly denied any knowledge of a road running east.

Though the Sakhi project did not suit me at all, I pretended to fall in with it, and they agreed to show us the road for forty rupees. I then told them, "This plan is all right, but it is a pity you could not show a road towards China, as in that case I would have given you more than double." They then retired, but reappeared in about an hour, saying that after consultation amongst themselves they had discovered that there was a road running east towards China, and were willing to make a bargain to take us ten marches along it. After much talking, during which they became quite oppressive in their friendliness, patting me on the back, and examining everything in the tent protesting all the time that they were not straightforward at first, as they thought we were the advanced guard of an army, and that now they meant to be honest with us, a bargain was concluded.

This is a great country for game; in the broken ground close to the river hares swarmed; antelope were to be seen in every direction, and *Ovis ammon* skulls lying about denoted that the living animals were to be found in the neighbouring hills.

Winds and clouds steady from west.

18th July, Camp 10; 14 miles, 16,874 feet.—Accompanied by our new guides we started east. The Ladakhi, who evidently knew nothing of the country we were now entering, was dismissed with a reward of a bigger sum than he had ever seen; on receiving it he burst into tears, and dropping on to his knees embraced my feet. On the road, seeing some yaks close by, I went after them, but the style of shooting one gets in this country is terribly demoralising, and instead of making a regular stalk, I presumed too much on their tameness, approached carelessly, only to be spotted by an old cow who gave the alarm, after which they all bolted. But an antelope, two hares, and a goose being bagged, we had abundance of meat.

19th July, Camp 11; 14 miles, 17,274 feet.—After travelling for a mile or two our guides stopped, and said that here two roads branched off—one going south-east to Hor Chang, by which Dokthol is reached in fourteen days, and on which we would meet people in four days' time; the other going straight east across a country they called Aru, where there was a large lake. I decided to take the latter route, though they tried hard to induce me to take the more southerly one, and could only be induced to show us the easterly route by offers of a larger reward than they would receive for the more southerly one. After concluding the bargain we shook hands, and they made great protestations of faithfulness.

The whole of the valley up which we travelled was littered with kiang and antelope, while the hills were dotted all over with yaks. Spotting a fine bull, all by himself, I went after him, taking a lesson from the result of my carelessness the day before, and approaching cautiously, got an easy shot, and bowled him over. On rejoining the caravan I found that the doctor had shot an antelope. To the north a fine snowy range was seen with one particularly fine peak.

This neighbourhood is evidently much frequented by nomads, though we met nobody, as numerous sheep-pens were to be seen.

20th July, Camp 12; Aru, 17,176 feet.—On waking up in the morning I was informed by the caravanbashi that the Khamba people were showing bad faith, and in spite of their promises and oaths of the day before, refused to go across Aru, on the grounds that they would be too long absent, and that in their absence Chukpas (brigands common to these parts) might attack their tents. I called them up and reproached them with faithlessness in going back on a bargain they had shaken hands over, and then having shown them the money I had got out as first instalment of the promised reward, ostentatiously put it back in a bag, saying, "All right, we can find our own way." The sight of the money aroused their cupidity, and my caravanbashi judiciously remarking at the same time that "Sahibs don't come this road every day," their scruples were overcome, and they renewed their protestations of the day before, adding thereto a considerable number of oaths.

Over a pass 17,876 feet, and then down a long narrow valley which suddenly debouches on Lake Aru Cho (17,150 feet),—a fine sheet of water running north and south, salt like nearly all the Tibetan lakes, and of a deep blue colour. To the south-west and north-west some fine snowy mountains rise up into the blue sky, while on the east low undulating barren-looking hills are seen. In every direction antelope and yak in incredible numbers were seen, some grazing, some lying down. No trees, no signs of man, and this peaceful-looking lake, never before seen by a European eye, seemingly given over as a happy grazing ground to the wild animals. A sportsman's paradise.

After emerging from the valley we turned north

up the side of the lake, and about two miles farther on came to a pool of fresh water, where we camped.

Camp 13; 14 miles, 17,276 feet.—We continued our way up the west side of the lake over a plain lying between the water and the mountains covered with grass and flowers. On the road a yak, which was sleeping in a hollow, jumped up under our feet, and gave the dogs a great run. The guides said that the last lake we passed is called Horpa Cho, and that from there a road runs across Hor to Polu. It may be so, or it may not, a Tibetan's having said so being hardly evidence.

22nd July, Camp 14; 21 miles, 17,701 feet.—Heading round the north edge of Lake Aru Cho, we crossed a neck of land with another lake, or rather the nearly dried-up remnants of a lake, interspersed with patches of salt, on our north. Then crossing a ridge we came down on a pool of brackish water, where we camped. Lots of argols about, so we were well off as regards fuel.

CHAPTER III

DESERTED BY OUR GUIDES

23rd July, Camp 15; 9 miles, 17,501 feet.—I was woke up at 4 A.M. by Kallick, the caravanbashi, with the astounding news that the Khamba men had deserted. Search was made and the tracks of their horses found, but it was impossible to follow them, as they could go much faster than we could. Things now seemed in a bad way. Here we were in a trackless waste, amidst a maze of mountains, no one to show where water or grass was to be found, or how to steer to reach a more hospitable country. If ever I meet those Khamba men again I am much afraid that the Christian virtue of forgiveness will be forgotten and they will have a bad quarter of an hour. However, the chance of meeting them was rather small, so vowing vengeance against them was of little use. The only thing to do, now we were without guides, was to go straight ahead. So we started off, down a valley in which a remarkably fine bull yak was grazing, but I felt too anxious to care about sport, and as regards meat, we had ample, so he was left alone. The valley we were following led into a much larger one, running east and west. We turned up it, keeping a look-out for water; soon a pool was found which to my great joy turned out to be fresh. So I gave the word to halt though we had only come nine miles, as it was impossible to say how much farther we might go before finding water again, and the animals were showing signs of over-work. Giving our Khamba friends credit for any amount of treachery, we took care to pitch the camp in a good strategical position, and at night took revolvers to bed with us. That they did not attack was owing, I have not the slightest doubt, to the way in which they had seen us knock over antelope. The fact that we were peaceful travellers who had paid them to serve us would carry little weight in their counsels. Near our camp we found signs of human beings having been there, such as wooden tubs and sticks used in gold-washing, two broken earthen pots, a piece of cloth, some traps for catching antelope, and a grave. Judging from appearances, the place must have been abandoned a long time ago. No recent signs of human beings were to be seen.

24th July, Camp 16; 17 miles, 17,501 feet.— Kept on up a valley passing on the south of a lake to the north of which was a fine snowy peak. On the road a number of pools, all more or less salt, were passed, but where we camped there was a spring of fresh water. All over the country there are patches of saline efflorescence, and the sides of the stream beds coming down from the hills, dry at this time of year, were covered with it.

25th July, Camp 17; 13 miles, 17,600 feet.—We made a late start owing to some of the ponies having strayed in the night. Getting up in the morning and finding ponies missing is terribly exasperating, especially when, as in this case, orders had been given the night before to tie them up in anticipation of making a start by daybreak at the latest. After proceeding a short distance an opening to our right disclosed to view a large grassy plain which we struck across in an east-south-east direction. In the afternoon I went about two miles to one side of the caravan, keeping a parallel course and looking out for fresh water. Finding a pool in a hollow, I tied my handkerchief on the end of an alpenstock and signalled to them: they changed direction at once and soon were on the spot. We had hardly got our tents up when a squall, accompanied by a little rain, was upon us. Similar storms, all coming from the south-west, had been seen about during the day, but we had been fortunate in missing them, and this one expended most of its force just south of us. Close to our camp there was a colony of bees living underground, with little holes on the surface through which they passed backwards and forwards.

26th July.—Halted. During the night we were treated to alternate storms of snow and rain, and when morning broke a thick mist hung over the country, making travelling an impossibility. So we spent the day overhauling pack-saddles. The storms, all coming from south-west or west, continued during the day.

27th July, Camp 18; 18 miles, 16,837 feet.—Another stormy night. On getting up I was distressed to find that the inclemency of the weather had killed one of the ponies, a good working beast whose loss we felt. During the time we were loading up, it snowed heavily, and I felt much inclined to countermand the order to march and halt another day; as finding one's way in a mountainous country without guides is difficult enough in clear weather, but in a snowstorm almost impossible. However, the sun appeared just in time, and we started thinking we were to have a fine day, but we had not gone far before another snowstorm, accompanied by thunder, was on us. Fortunately, in the interval between the storms I had ascended a ridge and taken compass bearings of what ought to be our road, otherwise we might have meandered aimlessly about the wide plain-like valley we were on until the snow lifted. As it was, when the snow stopped, we found ourselves close to a lake with a stream flowing into it, which gave an abundant supply of fresh water, so we camped.

These storms nearly always came from south or south-west, and in the day-time brought rain and at night snow. Occasionally lighter clouds came from the north or east, bringing snow in every case. The ponies were a great deal knocked up, continually lying down, and could only be induced to rise with difficulty.

OUR CARAVAN ON THE MARCH.

The bad weather took a great deal out of them, and the loads, being wet, were much heavier than they formerly were.

28th July, Camp 19; 11 miles, 16,762 feet.—A fairly easy march up an open valley with lots of grass about. On the way we passed marks of a camp not more than a month old, and where we camped there were signs of shepherds having been there, but the marks were several years old. Tibetan sand-grouse[1] were nesting, and on any one approaching their nests, fluttered slowly off, adopting the tactics excelled in by the plover tribe for drawing the intruder away.

29th July, Camp 20; 17 miles, 17,082 feet.—After keeping up a valley for some distance, we turned south into a nullah, where at least forty wild yak were grazing. West wind and very cloudy, but for a wonder we got neither snow nor rain, though some fell on all sides of us.

30th July.—Halted. During the night six donkeys and eighteen ponies disappeared, so there was nothing to do but stop and send men out to search. I much feared that Chukpas (brigands) had done the deed, although no tracks of men were to be seen. But that might be accounted for by their coming and going mounted, in which case their tracks would not have been discernible from our own ponies' tracks and only with difficulty distinguished from kiangs' tracks. My principal reason for thinking it was the work of Chukpas was the disappearance of the donkeys, who

[1] See page 294.

never before had shown an inclination to stray; on the contrary, they had invariably been a trifle too friendly at night, huddling together on the lee side of a tent and getting mixed up in the ropes in a way that threatened to bring the whole thing down with a run. Another suspicious fact was that a few nights previously Dr. Thorold felt sure he heard a man not far from us whistle; all hands were aroused at once, and the Chukpas, if they were about, did not attack; but it looked as if we were being followed, and now the disappearance of the animals seemed very like a confirmation.

I had come to the conclusion that, taken all round, an explorer's life is not altogether free from anxiety. Before going to bed that night it was arranged that search parties were to be sent out by daybreak; the men to be mounted on the best of our remaining animals, and to take provisions with them. It was a very annoying fact that the missing animals were all our best ones, those remaining being mostly on the point of breaking down altogether. Just after turning in it came on to blow very hard from the west, and though the pegs were weighted down with stone, boxes, bags of grain, etc., we momentarily expected the tents to be blown down. Sleep was out of the question during the first part of the night; but about midnight the storm moderated, and we managed to doze off.

Towards evening eight ponies were brought in, having been found in a valley to the south: this left me more puzzled than ever. If the Chukpas had taken the missing animals, they would most probably have held on to the lot, while if the animals had strayed, they would most probably have stuck together. On the whole, I still felt inclined to think it was the work of Chukpas, and that the animals recovered were some that had been driven up a side nullah to put us off the scent; another theory was that they had been enticed away by kiang.

Next evening, of the five men who had gone to search, only two had returned, and I was getting anxious about the others. One man, who had ascended the hills lying to the south of us, reported that on the other side there was a large plain with a lake in the middle of it, but no signs of inhabitants. On the third day, to my great joy, one of the absent men turned up, bringing the donkeys; he reported that the two other men were on the missing animals' tracks and wanted provisions sent after them. This was promptly done. To keep our larder full I went out and shot an antelope, cutting its throat, after shooting it, in orthodox Mussulman fashion; but when I returned to camp, opinion was much divided as to whether the animal was thus rendered lawful or not; some of the men maintaining that the ceremony having been performed by a Christian, it was of no avail; while others maintained that as long as it was done in proper form and the orthodox formula repeated, it did not matter who did it. The sticklers had to pay for their prejudices by doing without meat—a thing they disliked intensely.

On the fourth day all the missing animals, with the exception of one mule and four donkeys, were brought in; the men, who were much knocked up, reported having found them about three ordinary marches to the north at a place where there was a fresh-water lake about three days long, and innumerable yak. The pack-saddles were much knocked about, so to mend them and rest the men I decided to halt another day, which I determined to utilise by ascending a hill lying to the south of us in hopes of being able to map in some of the country on the far side.

This I did, and reached a height of considerably over 20,000 feet, but only with great difficulty, as the ground was covered with loose shale which gave with every step, and more than doubled the exertion. On the road a herd of *Ovis ammon* was passed, and on the far side of the hill numbers of yak were grazing, but the view was so completely obstructed by another hill that I failed to get any view and returned to camp very tired and disappointed. Rain fell at intervals during the day. Towards evening the missing mule came trotting into camp by himself, but there was no sign of the four donkeys, so I determined to march without them.

4th August, Camp 21; 15 miles, 16,482 feet.—Along the bed of a stream the whole day. Lots of grass. Bitterly cold wind.

5th and 6th August, Camp 22; 20 miles, 16,282 feet.—A long march up a valley at least 15 miles wide. On the north there was a fine snowy range running east and west. We saw no water all day, but towards evening, seeing some wild yak sitting down on a hill-side about 2 miles off, and thinking that they could not be far from water, I steered towards them, and found the herd, numbering forty-four, were all round several fine springs of fresh water. Close by there were some sheep-pens and cooking-places, but apparently they had not been used for a long time.

On the pools formed by the springs numbers of bar-headed geese[1] were sitting. They were just too young to fly, and with an expenditure of four cartridges nine were secured; they came in handy, as they gave us a pleasant change from our usual menu of stewed antelope.

We caught some locusts of a deep chocolate brown, quite a different kind from the ordinary Indian variety.

At night, in order to prevent their straying, I had all the ponies likely to do so hobbled, but it appeared to be of little avail, as in the morning it was discovered that several of the hobbled ones had gone off. As by the time they were recovered it was too late to march, we halted for the day and went for a stroll in the afternoon, shot several hares, saw more signs of nomads, and found an eagle's nest, round

[1] See page 300.

which the ground was covered with antelope bones, many of them split.

7th and 8th August, Camp 23; 23 miles, 16,082 feet.—Along a valley, in which there were many springs and fresh-water pools, but after we had marched about 6 miles they ceased, and it was not until 5.30 P.M. that we found water again. One horse knocked up completely, and even without a load failed to keep up with the caravan. During the day we had alternate squalls of rain and hail, and at night a hurricane set in, blowing one of the tents down; about midnight it moderated and heavy rain fell. During the storm several ponies, though hobbled, disappeared, and were not found until 11 A.M., thus necessitating another halt; not that I minded much, as round our camp the country was covered with grass, and a good feed would set them all up. I have never seen in Asia such a good imitation of an English meadow. One of our men picked up an ancient arrow-head.

9th August, Camp 24; 18 miles, 15,799 feet.—After ascending a ridge a lake came in sight, with incrustations of salt all round the edge. As the caravan drivers had been out of salt for five days, and about one ounce remained of that put aside for our personal use, we sent a man to get some; however, it turned out to be intensely bitter and quite uneatable. From the ridge a snowy range, stretching north and south, was seen straight in front of us, apparently blocking up the road, and I began to fear

A CAMP.

that after coming along so well we had got into a *cul de sac.*

In the evening we were treated to another storm of wind and rain from the west, and our tents were flooded.

10th August; 13 miles, 15,999 feet.—In the morning everything was soaking wet, and half an inch of water was standing in the tents; to give them a chance of drying we delayed starting for an hour or so after the sun was up, but still they were not anything like dry when we loaded. The country on the road appeared to be changing its character; outcrops of red and yellow sandstone appeared, and generally the landscape assumed a more Ladakh-like appearance. I sincerely hoped that this did not mean that grass was going to become scarcer, as, if it did, we should have been in a very bad way owing to the state our animals were already in from hard work and insufficient food. Showers from the west at intervals during the day as usual.

11th August, Camp 26; 12 miles, 16,074 feet.—After we had done 12 miles it looked as if the hills in front had effectually closed in on us; so, as water was found close by, I gave the word to halt, and started off for a *col*, which promised a good view for reconnoitring. Just as I got to the top, after two hours' hard climbing, a thick drenching Scotch mist, in which it was impossible to see more than two or three hundred yards, came on, and I was forced to return, no wiser than when I started.

12th August, Camp 27; 11 miles, 17,351 feet.—My reconnaissance of the day before having been quite futile, I was much puzzled at starting as to which way to go. However, nothing was to be gained by remaining where we were, so we went straight ahead, and after marching for five hours seemed more hopelessly entangled than ever. In the ravine were the remains of an old village, which apparently had been pretty large; the houses had been built partly underground, the Irishman's plan of raising the roof by sinking the floor apparently having been in vogue. But the puzzle was how they had been roofed, as timber cannot possibly be found anywhere near, and amongst the ruins there was no wood to be seen. Possibly tents were pitched over them.

Lots of gazelle (goa) were to be seen about; they are infinitely more knowing than either antelope or yak, and in the most out-of-the-way parts of Tibet promptly made off on seeing the caravan, as if they were accustomed to being shot at regularly.

13th August, Camp 28; 21 miles, 16,526 feet.—Started off by crossing a pass, and after that descended into a valley. As the country in front was most unpromising, and no signs of water were to be seen, we turned south, and late in the afternoon found a pool of water lying south-west of our line, which turned out to be fresh, so we camped close to it. On the east side of the pass a flock of choughs was seen, the first we had met since leaving Ladakh.

14th August, Camp 29; 16 miles, 16,551 feet.—Up a barren valley with gravelly soil, covered with saline efflorescence, until 2 P.M., when a small crater containing a spring was discovered, and we camped. Fine all day, but in the evening rain fell.

15th August, Camp 30; 14 miles, 16,907 feet.—The rain continued at intervals all night, and we started in a downpour which lasted till midday, when it cleared up. As usual a pass had to be crossed, and on the other side of it a large pond of fresh water, almost rising to the dignity of a lake, was found. Antelope, yak, and goa were grazing all round, and we found horns of both *Ovis ammon* and burhel. An excellent pony that had always headed the caravan, and was known as "the Commandant," died from exhaustion on this march.

16th August, Camp 31; 12 miles.—The way ponies manage to stray when hobbled is marvellous. We got up in the morning and found several that had been hobbled in such a manner as to make straying apparently an impossibility, had disappeared, and as they were not recovered before noon we made a late start, sincerely trusting that water would be found before dark; but as dusk was setting in, no signs of water were to be seen. We tried digging, but were unsuccessful, and then pushed on again. Just as it became too dark to go on any further, a snow squall struck us; we soon had the tents pitched, and a kettle filled with snow was on the fire. Dr. Thorold, however, had gone after some goa just before the snow set in, and had not rejoined the caravan, so I fired several shots, and guided by them he managed to find the camp.

17th August, Camp 32; 10 miles, 16,647 feet.—Once more the ponies strayed in the night. It was really a puzzle to know what to do about them; they had to be allowed to graze freely in the night, or else they would have been unable to march in the day, so tying them up was out of the question, and hobbling seemed of little use. The consequence of their straying was that once more we were obliged to make a late start.

As soon as the sun came out, the snow that had fallen during the night disappeared, and though there were showers all day, the ground never seemed to show any signs of it, drying extremely quickly when the sun came out.

August 18th, Camp 33; 14 miles, 16,747 feet. — Starting with snow on the ground we ascended a pass, and on reaching the top saw a huge mass of mountains apparently blocking the way straight in front. However, staying on the top of the pass was bitterly cold work and could do no good, so we descended following the bed of a stream. This grew perceptibly smaller as we advanced, showing decided signs of vanishing altogether, so we camped as far down as we could find sufficient water.

August 19th; 17 miles, 16,767 feet.—On this day the weather changed a good deal, the wind went round to the east and the clouds vanished. The range of mountains that the day before apparently had closed the way to the east, was still in front of us. However, what looked like a pass was seen toward the south, so we steered in that direction, surmounted it, and then were able once more to resume an easterly course. From the summit a fine lake was seen towards the north-east. Of our flock of ten sheep only one was alive, and it was to be kept in reserve in case we might some day be really short of food, a contingency which, considering that we had just shot three antelopes on the march, and game apparently was not getting scarcer, seemed far off.

August 20th, Camp 35; 17 miles, 16,167 feet. — After marching for a few miles, ascending all the time, we suddenly found ourselves on the outer edge of a plateau. To the south no mountains were visible, and straight in front of us the hollow was filled up with clouds, hiding mountains no doubt; still they must have been very much smaller than those behind us. As we descended, goa, antelope, burhel, and great numbers of hares were seen.

August 21st, Camp 36; 9 miles, 15,967 feet. — We were awakened in the night by the heavy rain beating against our tents. Towards morning it changed to snow, and though the ponies had not strayed far, finding them was rather a difficult matter, it being impossible to discover objects more than a hundred yards distant. About

10 A.M. it cleared up, and we marched; the mountains in front completely blocked the way, so it became a question of going either north or south; as a stream flowed south, I decided to go in that direction, considering it preferable to descend than to ascend — and besides it looked as if the valley would take a turn to the east. On the road we had several showers of sleet straight in our faces,

TEAPOT FROM TIBET.

and only with difficulty could the ponies be induced to face it; so we necessarily progressed very slowly. In the afternoon the sky became more and more threatening, and although we had only come nine miles, I judged it best to get under cover as soon as possible; so we camped, and no sooner were the tents up than the rain and sleet came down harder than ever. Owing to all the argols we could find being absolutely sodden, it was only with great difficulty that fire enough to cook some food was got. Fortunately a few dryish twigs, of a kind of heath, were found, that served to start the fire; the argols alone would never have burnt. I held an inspection of the commissariat, and found only enough grain to give the animals about a breakfast-cupful each and ten days' suttoo (tsampa) for the men; so I decided to hold the grain as a reserve and put all hands on considerably reduced rations.

CHAPTER IV

MEETING WITH NOMADS

August 22nd, Camp 37; 14 miles, 15,547 feet. — More rain fell during the night, but it cleared up in the morning, and as I did not care to put our tents, in the heavy sodden condition they were in, on the enfeebled animals, we delayed starting to let them dry.

After marching three or four miles we were all astounded by coming on the tracks of a herd of sheep, five horses, and a man; probably there would be more men with the party on the horses. The tracks were not more than a few hours old; the heavy rain that had fallen during the night would have obliterated any of the previous day's tracks. As we were running short of food and felt very much the want of a guide, I sent two men to follow up the tracks, and to obtain, if possible, sheep, flour, ghi,[1] salt, and a guide; if the latter was not procurable, they were to find out how far it was, in every direction, to an inhabited country. Knowing the uncertain character of these nomads, the two men

[1] Clarified butter.

took arms, but I instructed them to avoid getting into a row and only fire in case of dire necessity, to return as quickly as possible, and they would find the camp at the first water we came to. Having sent the two men off, we continued our route which lay across a low ridge of hills, which were cut up in a way that indicated a fairly heavy rainfall. On descending we found a spring in a ravine and camped beside it. Although I should have liked, owing to the scarcity of provisions, to have pushed on farther, in consideration of the two detached men I decided to halt. To add to our other troubles game was becoming much scarcer, though the existence of animals was shown by the head of a fine *Ovis ammon* lying close to the spring.

By nightfall there was no sign of the missing men, and I had a lamp put on one hill close to the camp and a fire lit on another, in order to serve as guides should they be wandering about in the dark. However, they did not turn up, and after spinning out the time until late, taking latitude observations, a difficult matter owing to the number of clouds about, I turned in, feeling very uneasy about the men.

August 23rd, Camp 38; 6 miles, 15,353 feet.—In the morning there were still no signs of the two men, so I climbed a neighbouring hill, from which a good view of the plain on the east was obtained. Except a few kiang, not a living thing was to be seen, so I returned to camp and sent two men to erect a flag extemporised out of a shirt and an alpenstock on the top of the pass to the west of us, and then sat down to an excellent breakfast consisting of stewed hare. All through the expedition hares and antelope did us yeoman's service in the commissariat line.

Soon after we had finished breakfast, the men at the flagstaff were discovered to be gesticulating wildly, having evidently sighted the absentees, who shortly afterwards arrived. They had followed the Changpas' (nomads living on the Chang, not to be confused with Chukpas, brigands) tracks for some miles, and at last had come in sight of them. The Changpas, who differ from the Khamba nomads by wearing pigtails, with the dread of strangers that seems the universal rule in these wilds, endeavoured to escape; but finding it impossible to do so unless they abandoned their flocks, and also gaining courage on seeing that their pursuers were so few, halted, turned round, and lighting the matches of their firelocks threatened to fire if the advance was continued. Kallick, the caravan driver, who spoke Tibetan, then began to parley with them, and a mutual laying down of arms was agreed to. Kallick then promised a good price if they would bring some sheep and butter to the camp, and also that if any man would guide us to a place where supplies were procurable he would be well rewarded. However, the Tibetan, who is the most suspicious person in the world, would have none of it. "Show us the money and we will see what can be done," was the only answer that could be got out of them, so the two men, not having sufficient money with them, turned back to rejoin the caravan, but being benighted on the way, had to sleep out with but little food and no fire. In the morning they saw the flag and thus found the camp. According to their account the country where the Changpas were camped was quite different in character; chukar, they said, a bird we never saw in Tibet proper, abounded. They also averred that they saw in the distance two monkeys; but the presence of monkeys in a treeless and almost barren country seems to me an anomaly that cannot be considered proved until one has been shot or at least seen by a European.[1]

After they had breakfasted and drunk an inordinate amount of tea, tired as they were, I decided to send them back armed with rupees to try and do a "deal" for some sheep. Matters were getting serious; there was no meat in camp, and a careful search of the country with field-glasses failed to disclose a single head of game. After sending them off we moved to a pool of water six miles distant, situated in the middle of a flat plain, where it was agreed they were to rejoin us.

A fine day, with masses of clouds (cumulus) coming up from the west.

[1] Since writing the above, I have seen that M. Bonvalôt mentions having seen monkeys in similar country, but the description he gives of them applies much more to the Marmot tribe than the Quadrumana.

In the morning there was no sign of the two men, but about 4.30 P.M. they returned and stated that on reaching the Changpas' camp they had had a long talk with an old man who appeared to be the head of the party. He said that the sheep were all out grazing, and that by the time they returned it would be too late to take them over the same evening, but that they would be handed over in the morning. Butter and salt they were also willing to sell, and samples of the former were produced by the women. As regarded a guide, the old man volunteered to go himself for a hundred rupees. At night, both parties being mutually suspicious of each other, my men retired to a distance of about half a mile, where they spent the night. In the morning they went to get the promised sheep. On arrival at the camp they were met by the old man, who professed himself willing to carry out all he had promised the previous evening. Suddenly, while they were talking, sixteen or seventeen men, assuming a threatening aspect towards both them and the old man, appeared, and after a deal of shouting, fired a very wild volley, the bullets going in every direction. One of them, however, broke a leg of the old man's horse. My orderly raised his carbine to return the fire, but the old man seized hold of the barrel, imploring him not to do so, as in case of any one being hurt the whole punishment after our departure would be visited upon him for having dealings with strangers. He also told them that they must go at once; that delay was of no use, as, owing to the arrival of these men, he dared not now supply anything. So both the men returned to camp, my orderly in his retreat carrying off a bag of salt.

The character of all these Tibetan nomads, who appear totally independent of either China or Lhasa, is much the same—suspicious, greedy, and avaricious. They are extremely difficult to deal with. On this occasion I purposely did not go near them myself, as nearly all Asiatics are suspicious of Europeans, and my men alone could easily pass themselves off as merchants from Ladakh; but with the Tibetan of these parts it makes little difference who you are; towards strangers their conduct is always the same,—robbery, if they dare. Near our frontier it is easy to understand the suspicion and fear with which natives look on Europeans, but in Central Tibet the suspicion seems to rest on humanity in general, every party of nomads being frightened of every other party. Absence of the requisite pluck is the only thing that prevents them from being excellent brigands.

We were now in a worse plight than ever. The two days lost meant two days' provisions consumed. Nothing had been shot; as for the salt, having been some time without any, we were very glad to get it, but still a bag of flour would have been of considerably more value.

August 25th, Camp 39; 23 miles, 15,146 feet.—All hope of getting a guide having failed, we started to try and find a way to Tengri Nor, whence it would be easy to find a road to Shiabden Gomba or Talung Gomba, at either of which places supplies would be procurable. According to information picked up by the two men while in the Changpas' Camp, Tengri Nor was ten days distant. But in ten days, according to the nomads' way of travelling, an enormous stretch of country can be covered, and as we did not know the way, the chances were very much against our finding the most direct road; thus the ten days for us probably meant twenty. The day's march to where we found a pool of rain-water on some clayey impermeable soil was easy enough; but the food difficulty was getting serious. All our efforts to shoot something only resulted in a bag of three hares considerably smaller than English rabbits, and that was not much among eleven hungry men. The one Hindustani in the party having persuaded a certain number of men that it is not lawful to eat the flesh of an animal *hallaled*[1] by a Christian, was a great nuisance, as we often shot animals when at some considerable distance from the caravan, and by the time any of the Mussulman drivers could arrive to perform the ceremony, the animal had generally been dead some time. However, most of the men were willing, if not observed, to cut the throat any time after the animal's death, and on returning to camp to swear it was alive when the ceremony was performed. On

[1] Cutting the throat of an animal for food according to the Mussulman rites.

A TIBETAN SALUTATION.

one occasion I shot an antelope, and reaching camp an hour afterwards, pointed out the direction and sent a man to *hallal* it. Some hours afterwards he brought the animal into camp with its throat cut, and solemnly averred that he had found it alive.

While enjoying a cup of tea after a long march, suddenly five kiang hove in sight about two miles off. I was rather tired and disinclined to move, but meat had to be got somehow, so taking my rifle, I started after them. They were on an open plain, where a "stalk" was out of the question, so when about a quarter of a mile from them I began moving about in an oblique direction, gradually edging in. When I got within about 250 yards they took alarm, and slowly moved off in single file. Lying down, I had a steady shot, but they all galloped off apparently none the worse, when one of them, having gone a couple of hundred yards, pitched on its head and lay motionless. I rushed up and found a fine fat mare, meat for all our party for three days at least, probably for more. The bullet had struck behind the shoulder, too far back for the heart. I have never seen a wild animal with so much fat; the stomach was simply coated with it.

26th August, Camp 40; 25 miles, 15,171 feet.—A longish march up an open valley, which seemed to terminate in a ridge straight ahead of us. There was no water on the road, and in the afternoon I became anxious about it. However, just as we reached the ridge, an opening in it disclosed to view a valley at a lower level than the one in which we had been travelling, and where there were some pools of water and a flock of sheep. We moved down to the nearest pool, and camped about half a mile from the black tents of some nomads. Whether they were Chukpas (brigands) or Dokpas (ordinary nomads) was a question we were rather doubtful about. However, brigands or not, we wanted water, and had to camp near them. I wished to go over to their tents myself and see if we could get some supplies, but was persuaded not to by the caravan drivers, who said that if a European was seen all hopes of assistance would be at an end; so I relinquished the idea and allowed two of the men to go alone. Late in the evening they returned, reporting that the strangers, who were Dokpas, and did not wear pigtails like the Changpas we had previously met, had received them with levelled matchlocks. However, by assurance of friendly intentions, their hostility was overcome, and the two men were invited into a tent to drink tea. The Dokpas excused themselves for the apparently hostile reception on the ground that they lived in great dread of the Chukpas, and had feared that we were a party of those gentlemen, but now saw their mistake. After drinking tea my men broached the subject of supplies, and were told we should receive whatever we wanted in the morning, but that it was now too dark to inspect the sheep. The question of a guide was then brought forward, but they would have none of it, saying that if they supplied a guide they would be punished for bringing strangers into the country. They were also very diplomatic in their replies to questions as to the direction and distance of various places, giving answers obviously intended to deceive. As nothing further was to be got out of them, the two men returned to camp.

Camp 41; 4 miles, 15,346 feet.—This place is called Sira Nagmo. In the morning with the first streak of day Kallick and Abdul Rahman, the two men who had gone the previous evening, started off again for the Dokpas' camp. Arrived there they found the party packing up preparatory to moving. After a lot of bargaining, some butter, some suttoo (tsampa, parched barley, ground), and five sheep were procured, the latter at three rupees each, and the suttoo and butter in exchange for some coral beads, the coral beads being relatively valued more than the rupees.

After the bargain was concluded, they expressed a belief that there were Europeans in the party, and threw doubts on Kallick's assertion that we were a party of pilgrims from Ladakh, travelling to Tengri Nor on a pilgrimage, and refused to deliver up the articles bargained for until satisfied with their own eyes that there were no Europeans in the party. So two of them started for our camp, bringing the butter, tsampa, and sheep with them. Kallick, being mounted, galloped ahead and reached us 500 yards in front of the Dokpas, so we had lots of time to change our things; and by the time they arrived Doctor Thorold, in ragged native garments holding a pony, looked as unlike a member of the medical profession as it is possible to look, while I, with borrowed plumes, played the part of a Mussulman merchant. On arrival, the Dokpas saluted by thrusting out their tongues, a mode of salutation I had never seen before, but I promptly thrust out mine. We then had a long conversation, in which they refused all my attempts to bribe them into furnishing a guide, but before departing they handed over all the supplies, being fully satisfied that there were no Europeans in the party. However, we made up our mind that in future it would be advisable always to wear native garments, as we might chance on some of these suspicious Tibetans at any moment. These Dokpas, unlike the Changpas, appear to be more or less subject to Lhasa. They also differ considerably in their diet, eating a certain amount of suttoo, whereas the Changpas practically live entirely on the produce of their herds and flocks.

The negotiation took up the whole of the forenoon, so we were unable to do a decent march, and camped at the first water met with. No sooner had we got into camp than the weather, which had been fine in the morning, changed, and heavy rain came up from the west.

28th August, Camp 42; 21 miles, 14,796 feet.—A long rise over a pass, and then a descent into a ravine where we found a spring and camped. On the road I saw what I took to be a nomad's tent, but, on getting nearer, it was discovered to be a stack of wool bound with ropes. No one was to be seen about.

The country was terribly cut up by ravines, far and away the worst we had encountered. How we were to find our way out of it seemed a puzzle. With unlimited time it would of course be easy, but our larder was not well enough furnished to allow of delay. The suttoo we had obtained from the Dokpas weighed 80 lbs., and altogether we had 140 lbs., not much amongst eleven men in a mountainous country without guides, and no certainty as to when more would be procurable.

29th August, Camp 43; 14,621 feet.—The country each side of the stream was so cut up by nullahs that it was quite impracticable, so we had to stick to the bed, though as it meandered about a great deal, geographically we made but little progress. At last we emerged on a valley running north and south, and as a stream flowed into it from the other side, we took advantage of the bed to maintain an easterly direction by following it up. It was a very short stream, and after a couple of miles or so we emerged on a plateau, where we thought our difficulties with the ravines were over. However, we had not gone far before we were brought up by a precipice, at the foot of which a large stream rising in the snowy range to the south was flowing. We had to march along the edge of the cliff for some little distance before a place at which it was possible to descend was found. On descending we found ourselves on the banks of the largest stream met with since leaving the Indus.

It was about 3 feet deep, and with a very strong current. All the animals got safely over, though one was very nearly drowned, having been knocked down by the current. The place we crossed at was eminently adapted for the purpose, the stream being split up into three or four branches; the greater part of it must be quite unfordable for ponies and mules, and earlier in the season I suppose it is absolutely impossible to get over anywhere.

After a general wringing of garments we marched up the bed of a tributary for a few miles, and camped about two miles from some nomads' tents. I at once sent some men over to obtain supplies; they returned shortly after dark, having been very successful, and bringing with them 80 lbs. of suttoo, 20 lbs. of wheat flour, and some butter, a great haul, and one which enabled the half-ration system to be succeeded by full rations. The Dokpas, amongst whom was a Lhasa official collecting tribute, had been most particular in their inquiries as to whether there were any English in the party, as they had heard a rumour that there was to be a war with the English. Of course they were told there were none, upon which they asked if we had a passport, and wanted to know if it was countersigned by the Rajah of Ladakh. One of my men, a gentleman who was always well to the fore when any lying had to be done, assured them everything was *en règle.* As the Rajah of Ladakh was deposed more than fifty years ago, it appears that news travels slowly in these parts.

In the course of conversation several geographical facts were elicited; Lhasa was twelve days distant, and on the road there was a place called Dhomra, at which an official of high rank was quartered. All the way inhabitants would be met, but if they suspected the presence of Englishmen there would be trouble. So there was nothing to do, much as we disliked it, but stick to our disguises until some responsible person was met with. The river we had just crossed flowed into Lake Chuksi Cho, which was a day's march distant, and so large that it took seven days to ride round it.

30th August, Camp 44; 13 miles, 14,796 feet.—In the early morning, as Dr. Thorold and myself were at breakfast, a Dokpa suddenly appeared, evidently having come to spy. We dived into our tent, and he was taken to the caravan driver's tent, where he was regaled with tea. During the time he was there he asked a lot of inconvenient questions. As soon as the unbidden guest had departed, we loaded up and started, crossing a pass and then descending into the bed of a stream which we followed up; while we were going along it, three Tibetans appeared following us. I stopped and asked them what they wanted, and was told that they only wanted to know if we would buy some suttoo, so I allowed them to come on their promising to deal for it as soon as we camped. Presently, they were augmented by others who came dropping in by twos and threes until they outnumbered the men in the caravan; amongst them were four women. Happening to turn round, I saw that the women were being sent off, so thinking this a suspicious sign I halted and told the Tibetans that we were travelling under a passport, could not be interfered with, and would not allow them to come any farther. After a deal of palavering they were induced to halt, and eventually they turned back.

Amongst other information they told me that the Lhasa official had gone to call the Zhung or headman of the district, and that he would catch us up in a few days.

From our camp a road, passing between two lakes and then over a pass in a southerly direction, led, according to them, to Lhasa, but next day we discovered that they had said so only to mislead us; it really led to Tashi Lunpo.

CHAPTER V

IN THE NEIGHBOURHOOD OF LHASA

31st August, Camp 45; 20 miles, 15,621 feet.—Early in the morning a poor mendicant Lama came over to our tents to ask for charity and also probably to spy. He said that we had been wrongly informed as to the roads, the one to the south leading to Tashi Lunpo, and to reach Lhasa it was necessary to go through a depression in the hills to the east. As this was more in accordance with my own observations I came to the conclusion that he was telling the truth, and so we started off in that direction. The valley was studded with black tents, and herds of sheep and tame yak were grazing in every direction. Goa and kiang were also to be seen, but the former were very wild, the latter were in troops and decidedly inquisitive. On reaching the head of the valley we followed the bed of a rivulet fed by springs which took us on to some high plateau-like ground, where we met once more our old friends, the Tibetan antelope; we had not seen any for some days, and it is evident that they very rarely descend below 15,000 feet, and are decidedly scarce below 16,000 or 17,000 feet. In the night heavy rain fell, coming from the west.

1st September, Camp 46; 17 miles, 15,348 feet.—On leaving camp we went through a narrow defile that opened out on a wide valley in which was an enormous lake. As we were approaching it, three mounted men caught us up, one of whom appeared to be a sort of headman. He wanted to know all about us, and was not at all satisfied on being shown the Chinese passport, as he said that the year before two Russians (by whom I presume he meant the two French travellers, M. Bonvalôt and Prince Henri of Orleans) had come into the country, also provided with a Chinese passport; that immediately afterwards information had come from China that a passport had inadvertently been issued, but that no notice was to be taken of it and all Europeans were to be rigidly excluded. He then wanted us to halt while he communicated with some of his superiors. This I refused to do, and at the same time told him that our only reason for taking the Lhasa road was the necessity for obtaining provisions, our real intention being to go to China, and if he would supply our wants, we would continue travelling east and would pass to the north of Lhasa. However, he would not agree to this, and said he had heard from Lhasa that an English invasion of Tibet by the Chang was expected, and he suspected our party of being the advance guard.

Near our camp there were three upright stones

resembling those on Salisbury Plain, and close to them were the foundations of several rectangular stone houses. I was surprised at seeing them, as the highest flights in the architectural line that we had hitherto seen were some old sheep-pens. In the evening more Tibetans arrived, and having pitched their camp a little distance off, came over to try and induce us to halt, but being unsuccessful in their endeavours, departed.

2nd September, Camp 47 ; 18 miles, 15,773 feet. —Soon after leaving the last camp we found ourselves on the banks of a large stream flowing into the lake. Although it was cut up into many branches, it took us some time to find a ford, and then we only got over with difficulty, all our bedding and baggage getting wet. Another stream farther on, though it did not hold nearly as much water, was almost as difficult to cross, owing to the stony nature of the bottom and the force of the current. After crossing it, we turned up a valley on the south and camped. While we were pitching tents a number of men, all armed with sword and matchlock, came up, and going a little ahead of us, camped. They were followed by some more who camped on the other side, thus hemming us in completely. I sent two men to ask what they wanted, and received an answer that this was their country, and they were moving about in it—an answer to which it was impossible to take exception.

Camp 48 ; 12 miles, 16,148 feet.—After a night

of very heavy rain we continued our way up the valley. Passing the nomads' camp *en route*, they all rushed out with a great sticking-out of enormous tongues. I asked the one who seemed chief of them, a little wizened old "Black Dwarf" with a limp, if he would sell provisions, and after a lot of bargaining obtained a maund of suttoo (82 lbs.) for the ridiculously exorbitant price of fifteen rupees. On leaving them the headman promised to catch us up soon, bringing with him a large stock of provisions. He was as good as his word about catching us up, but he brought no provisions, and his escort had mysteriously doubled in size. Next morning, as we were preparing to start, a delegate from the Dokpas' tent turned up, recommending that as our tents must be wet we should halt till they dried; as they had not been dry for five weeks, their being wet was not a consideration likely to influence our movements much, and I told him so.

He departed, and in his place the Black Dwarf appeared, petitioning that we would halt for a couple of hours or so in order to give a Zhung, or official, who was hourly expected, a chance of catching us up. As it was sleeting hard, and in any case loading up would take nearly an hour, I consented. Before an hour had elapsed the great man turned up, accompanied by a lesser light. He went to the Dokpas' tent, and sent four men to ask us who we were and what we wanted in the country; to this I answered that if he wanted to know, he had better come over himself, as

I was not going to be interrogated by menial servants. On receiving my message the great man, accompanied by the lesser light and a dozen of unwashed hangers-on, came over to our camp. I took them into my tent and seated them on yakdans, after which they rather abruptly opened the conversation by asking "Who are you and what do you want here?" In reply, I said, "We are English, we have come from Ladakh, are going to China, and here is our passport; we don't want to go to Lhasa, and have only come south to obtain provisions: give us provisions and a guide, and we will continue our journey east."

They answered us that if we attempted to proceed, they would be obliged to oppose us; as, if they did not do so, they would certainly lose their heads. If we fought and killed them, it was just as good as being executed in Lhasa. They were absolutely immovable in this resolve, and I have not the slightest doubt would have attempted to stop our progress by force had we resolved to go on at all hazards. So I judged it better to come to some understanding with them, and after arguing over every trifling point, and much circumlocution, the following treaty was drawn up:

(1) We were to be taken to a place three marches off in either an easterly or southerly direction, where water and grass were plentiful.

(2) Arrived there, we would halt fifteen days, in order to allow matters to be settled in

Lhasa, and allow any officials who might be sent to see us.

(3) During our halt we were to receive daily 1 sheep, 12 lbs. flour, 12 lbs. tsampa, and 1 lb. butter, to be supplied at a rate which they said was under market rates.

(4) The safety of ourselves and our property was guaranteed, and the value of anything stolen was to be paid to us.

After the treaty was drawn up, before they left, I gave them each a small present, and hinted at the possibility of other and more valuable ones being forthcoming in the event of matters being satisfactorily arranged.

They were both men of a very superior type to the wandering Dokpas; intellectually and physically they were fine men, and about both there was an air of pronounced individuality. As regards their dress, they wore the same kind of dingy red woollen garments ordinarily worn by Lamas; across the shoulder they had belts, on which were strung miniature shrines, about 7 inches by 4, containing prayers, etc. Their hair was in pigtails, much ornamented with turquoises, etc., and brushed well back from the head, quite a different style from the ordinary Tibetan fashion, where the pigtail is only an adjunct to a shock-like mass of hair, innocent of brush, comb, soap, or water. They made light of Chinese influence in Tibet, utterly ridiculing the idea of Chinese

TIBETAN EAR-RINGS.

supremacy and saying the only ruler in Tibet was the Deva Zhung (Central Government of Lhasa,—the term is also sometimes applied to the Talai Lama). In the evening very heavy rain fell, and as no dry argols were to be found, we had great difficulty about cooking anything, and were reduced to burning the ridge pole of a tent.

5th September, Camp 49; 23 miles, 15,523 feet.—Our friends, the Tibetan dignitaries, were not ready to start with us, evidently indulging in that luxury known in India as a "Europe morning," but a small boy was sent to show us the way towards the place where we had agreed to halt. Marching in the same direction as ourselves was an enormous caravan, consisting of about 400 yaks, 50 horses, and several thousand sheep. In reply to our inquiries we were told that they were a party of merchants, Chinese subjects, that their home was one and a half months distant, and that having brought goods into the country they had exchanged them for live-stock which they were now taking back. However, some of the Tibetan officials' followers who had caught us up, told a different story, saying that they were Chukpas (brigands), and that all the animals were the produce of industry in other paths than those of commerce, and the farther apart we camped the better. So, acting on this advice, after the wolves in sheep's clothing halted, we continued our march for another 8 miles and camped on the banks of a stream flowing into a large lake. Numbers of nomads' black tents were to be seen in every direction.

6th September, Camp 50; 30 miles, 15,423 feet.—A few miles after leaving camp 49 we crossed a narrow neck of land between two lakes, the northern one of immense size, while the southern one was of extremely irregular shape, having branches running up valleys in every direction, and islands, some of them fairly large, scattered about its surface. It was of singular beauty, to the south a high cone-shaped peak, capped with snow, threw its shadow across; but what made the great difference between it and other Tibetan lakes was the freshness of the water. Grass grows right down to the edge, and the invariable adjuncts of fresh water, gulls and terns, wheeling about and uttering cries, gave a feeling of life and animation contrasting strongly with the death-like solitude hanging over the salt lakes. It is almost impossible to get the correct names of places or lakes in Tibet, as every Tibetan lies on every occasion on which he does not see a good valid reason for telling the truth. Sometimes I have asked half a dozen men separately the name of a lake and received half a dozen different answers. The names I have put on my map are those in favour of which slightly more evidence was forthcoming than for others, but still some of them, including those of these lakes, may turn out to be erroneous when further explorations have made us better acquainted with the country.

We received a sheep on getting into camp as a first instalment of the treaty provisions, which looked as if our Tibetan friends judged it politic to carry out their part of the treaty. And the escort having increased to at least eighty men, it looked as if they were going to insist on our carrying out our part.

Camp 51, Gagalinchin; 28 miles, 15,560 feet.—After leaving our last camp we crossed a narrow neck of land, about the size of and somewhat resembling a railway embankment, with a lake on each side. A Tibetan, in the course of conversation with one of the caravan drivers, stated that the large lake on the north, of which we were continually getting glimpses and occasionally extended views, was called Tengri Nor by Mongols and Tengri Cho by Tibetans; but I fear he lied. However, whatever the right name might be, there was no doubt of its being a noble sheet of water, stretching out east and west to an enormous distance; it seemed more worthy to be called an inland sea than a lake. But, like all the Tibetan lakes, it showed signs of once having been larger than it is now; indeed some of the lakes appear to have dwindled to about half their original size. Between it and our camp were some large lagoons of fresh water fed by streams coming down from the hills.

The escort seemed to grow in size every hour. Parties pouring out from all the side valleys fell in and came on with us. Though possibly they were not all intended to form a guard of honour, I thought it best to regard them as such, and hugged myself with the idea that we were being treated as distinguished guests. They were a quaint-looking lot, with long rifles terminating in a prong-like rest, to one arm of which was attached a red flag, slung over their shoulders. Straight swords in scabbards encrusted with silver and studded with turquoises, stuck cross-ways in the front of their belts, prayer-wheels in hand, dirty sheepskin raiment, hats that must have been introduced by a designer of garments for a burlesque, shock heads, pigtails, short stirrups, and miniature steeds, all made up a picture that I longed to photograph, but judged it wise not to for fear of exciting their suspicions.

In accordance with the treaty, next day we halted, and I spent the forenoon inspecting the baggage animals. When the pack-saddles were removed, they presented a ghastly spectacle, nothing but skin, bones, and sores; the latter I attributed to a considerable extent to insufficient nutriment.

If any doubts had ever existed in my mind as to the superiority of mules over ponies, they were quite removed, as, though they were bad enough, the ponies were much worse. Although halting seemed very disagreeable, yet we should have been obliged to do so whether the Tibetans had insisted on it or not. But it was just as well to impress upon them that we only halted owing to the kindly feeling that sprang up in our bosoms on seeing men of such distinguished and benevolent mien.

From our camp a road ran southward to Lhasa where people were continually passing backwards and forwards; one party said they were going to meet the dignitary of high rank who was expected out to interview us. As my passport was for Chinese Turkistan and mountains to south and west, I anticipated that when read we would be allowed to go to Chinese Turkistan and nowhere else. The Tibetans sent over more supplies, consisting of a cake of brick tea, two pounds of butter and two sacks of dry argols, but no flour or suttoo, those things not having arrived. However, they came next day, and we were given in addition a cake of a sort of Tibetan cheese, which might have been wholesome, but certainly was not good. A plenipotentiary that I sent over to the Zhung's camp to fetch fuel, reported on returning that the old man had hinted that when permission came from Lhasa to proceed, he expected a trifling douceur in return for his trouble in providing a guide. So, rejoicing to find that he was civilised enough to understand the nature of a douceur, I sent a message that he need not fear on that score; indeed as my knowledge of Tibetans increased, my delicacy about suggesting gratuities decreased in arithmetical proportion.

In order to try and find out the real name of the big lake, I instructed a caravan driver to get into conversation with the passers-by on the road and find out from them. The whole of Tibet could not have been instructed to give false answers, so, barring the natural tendency of the people, there was nothing to prevent the real name being got at; but that natural tendency struck me as a pretty difficult obstacle, when he returned having interviewed several parties and got different names from each.

The Zhung paid us a state visit in the evening and was very pressing in his inquiries as to where we had first met inhabitants. Evidently the arrival of Europeans had not been as quickly reported as it should have been, and he wanted to punish the delinquents; but as we had been dressed in Ladakh raiment and the people always prefer to look at strangers from afar off, our not being noticed as Europeans was hardly to be wondered at.

Next day when we were starting off to pay a return visit to our friends, a messenger came over from their camp, asking us to postpone it, as they were very busy owing to important news having arrived. We were naturally curious as to what had happened, and the messenger showed no unwillingness to be communicative. It appeared that the Chukpas, whom we had passed on the road, not content with the enormous numbers of animals they had collected, had made another raid, and after killing several men had driven off 200 yaks, 50 horses and an enormous number of sheep. Such a state of affairs close to Lhasa was unheard off and occasioned great excitement. Meanwhile the Zhung was busy organising parties in order to endeavour to recover the stolen property. I suggested that as the Chukpas' herds were close by, the best plan would be to seize them, but it appeared that they had been lifted in Kangri, a country away to the east; and as the Deva Zhung received a tax on each head driven through the Lhasa country, they were regarded as inviolable. As the Chukpas on their part undertook not to raid in the country near Lhasa and had broken their bond, I should have thought the Lhasa people would have been justified in breaking theirs also, but the Zhung looked at it differently; his idea was that the fact of the Chukpas having committed a breach of good manners was no reason for his also doing so, but at the same time he would not hesitate to execute them if he got a chance.

A Lama came to visit us, and was very strong in information regarding the names of places and other geographical facts, but the names and the facts differed very considerably from those given by other people. On the whole I was inclined to think him fairly truthful. He called the big lake in front Garing Cho, the district we were in Naksung Sittok, and to the east lay Doba, Namru Sera, and Nakchu. In the latter Shiabden Gomba is situated, and from there two roads run towards China, one on the north to Sining, or as he called it, Gya Zilling, and a more southerly one of which he knew nothing. Chukpas abounded on the Sining road, and the general custom was for travellers to wait at Shiabden Gomba until several hundreds could be collected and then cross the dangerous zone together for mutual protection. From Namru a road runs to Lhasa, by which it would be possible to go straight into the sacred city without meeting a soul; but for us the Zhung and his small army put that out of the range of practical politics. Our arrival had created tremendous excitement. First of all rumours spread that an English army was coming, next that it was only a party of Chinese travellers, and lastly the true one, that we were English, and our objects peaceful.

These lesser lights of the Buddhist church seem much less bigoted in their hatred of foreigners than either the nomads or higher dignitaries; the one we met before most certainly put us on the right road when we were about to take the wrong, and this one struck me as being decidedly friendly.

Next day we paid the deferred visit to the Zhung and Kushok[1] Lama. Though their camp was only a quarter of a mile distant, it would have been undignified to walk, and as riding a mule is as good as a diploma of rank, the two most respectable-looking ones were saddled, and we rode over to where the Zhung's tent was pitched, amidst a dozen or so of the ordinary blackish nomads' pattern. The settlement, if such a term can be applied to nomads, all turned out to gaze at us; and as we dismounted the Zhung appeared and ushered us into a tent, of which one-half, made of rough sacking and open at the roof, was evidently intended to serve as kitchen and servants' quarters, while the other half, made of thin calico, and with carpets and cushions about, was evidently the drawing-room. As soon as we were seated a laboured conversation was started. Talking

[1] Kushok. The word is usually applied to an incarnation.

through an interpreter is not particularly lively at any time, but in this case it was terribly hard work, as the Zhung, being afraid of committing himself, gave most laconic answers. I was particularly anxious to find out something about the Chukpas and their raids, but the only thing I found out was that when pursued by the ordinary country-people they would often turn round and fight, but if pursued by soldiers from Lhasa they never fought. When taken, if convicted of having been concerned in a raid in which blood had been shed, they were executed; otherwise they were punished by flogging and imprisonment.

Soon after we had returned to our own camp, the Lama who had previously given information arrived, bringing one of higher rank with him. On entering my tent, according to Tibetan custom he presented me with a khatag, or scarf of greeting, a long white arrangement, generally of an extremely flimsy nature, though I have seen them made of beautiful silk. Their use is very general throughout Tibet, being invariably presented when making a call. He also presented some gur (molasses), cheese, and butter. After being seated, in the course of conversation he confirmed generally all the information given by the other Lama, and said that if we went by the Sining road we should probably get there before the heavy snowfall came, as it did not usually come before January. He suggested the Gya Lam[1] as an alternative route. It

[1] Gya Lam. Lam is the Tibetan for road, and Gya means Chinese.

ran from near Shiabden Gomba *vià* Bathang and Lithang to Tarsedo,[1] and was easy going all the way, with no danger to be apprehended from Chukpas, who seem ever present in Tibetan minds. A third road ran from Shiabden Gomba to Gya Kudo or Gyakundo, but it was so difficult as to be almost impracticable.

Close to our camp was a stream rising in some springs, and containing numbers of small fish, but the difficulty was how to catch them. Dr. Thorold was seedy, and wanted something in the way of luxuries, and here was a stream stiff with fish, and apparently no means of catching them. At last the difficulty was solved. In Dr. Thorold's tent were two pockets made of netting; these, augmented with sacking, were stretched between two alpenstocks, and were held by men in a narrow place, so as to let the water run over and through, not under. Mud was thrown into the water to discolour it, and two men drove the fish with sticks and stones down to the narrow place where the net was. Then, at a given signal, and with a forward and upward motion, it was thrown on to the bank, and a dozen fish was considered a poor catch. For the rest of the halt we had fish at every meal, and we dried some as well for the march.

Close to the camp burhel (*Ovis nahura*) were

The expression Gya Lam might be used for any road going to China, but this was evidently the chief China road.

[1] Tarsedo, called variously Darchendo, Tarsedo and Ta Chen Lu.

plentiful, and shikaring them helped to enliven the otherwise tedious halt. Goa were also to be seen, but they were on more open ground, and it was difficult to get a shot at them. Every day some provisions came over from the Tibetan camp. As regards butter, they seemed inclined to give us as much as we cared to take, but it was very dirty, and generally rancid, and being wrapped up in skins and sheep stomachs, hardly presented an appetising appearance.

On September 20th the man who had been sent into Lhasa came back, bringing some tobacco, red pepper, etc. The caravan drivers, who had not been able to enjoy the luxury of a smoke for some time, rejoiced exceedingly on receiving a ration each of the fragrant herb. A letter was also brought from a relative of one of the caravan drivers, a small trader in Lhasa, in which we were strongly advised to get out of the country by the road we had come as quickly as possible, or the consequences might be serious. I did not attach much importance to the letter, as I conjectured it had been written at the instigation of the Lhasa authorities, in order to intimidate us, and only showed what card they were going to play first, —bluster, and orders to return the way we had come.

After dark a man came to my tent offering to sell some fine flour. I gladly bought it, and afterwards discovered that he was the Zhung's cook, and it was quite possible he had stolen it from his master. However, I did not feel myself called upon to denounce him. Another man in the nomads' camp had a little rice, and was willing to sell it, but the price he asked was ridiculous, 4 annas a pound. Much as I would have liked to, I did not take it, as, had I done so, news would have spread that the foreigners were made of money, and a special tariff for their benefit would have been instituted.

During all the time we had been halting, preparations for the great men who were expected from Lhasa had been going on steadily. Carpets and articles to embellish tents arriving from Shildut, a place in a west-south-west direction, and provisions from Lhasa; and on September 24th the first of them arrived gorgeous in yellow silk robe and scarlet umbrella. On arrival he promptly sent a message asking me to halt three more days, as he had no power to settle matters himself, but a colleague was already on the road, and might be expected any day. To this I replied that I should be delighted to halt three more days—an answer that was the only one I could give considering the state of the animals, and I hoped he would come over and drink a cup of tea.

TEAPOT FROM TIBET.

CHAPTER VI

NEGOTIATIONS WITH LHASA OFFICIALS

On September 27th, the Kushok of Naksung, the expected colleague, turned up, and sent a man to call me over to his tent. I replied that if he wanted to see me he had better come to my tent; as I had waited twenty-one days for him, it was the least he could do. He came over as I knew he would, the message having been simply an attempt to see if I could be bullied. Like all high dignitaries, he rode a mule, and held a bright red umbrella over his head; the latter much puzzled my orderly, who could not make out whether it was to keep off the sun or the rain, there being no signs of either at the time. The other Lhasa swell and our two old friends also came with him. My tent was prepared for their reception by neatly-arrayed yakdans covered with scarlet blankets to serve as seats. As soon as all were seated, business was promptly opened by the question, "Who are you, and where do you come from?" I replied, that we were English travellers; we had intended to pass more to the north, but having run short of provisions, had steered towards the south, confident that, owing to the friendship existing between the British and Lhasa Governments, we should receive every assistance. They answered that Tibet was forbidden ground to all strangers; that the only thing they would permit us to do was to return at once the way we had come; and as for the friendship existing between the two governments, that was no reason why the people of both nations should not stick to their own countries. I then told them that it was of no use to continue talking if they were going to introduce the subject of returning the way we had come.

The Chinese passport they did not even want to see, as they said information had been received from Pekin that two passports had been issued, one to Englishmen and the other to Russians, but having been issued by mistake, they were not to be regarded as in any way valid; and even had no such information been received, it did not make any difference, as Tibet was in no way under China, and the Emperor had not the power to grant a passport for the Deva Zhung's territory. No delegate having come from the Amban, or Chinese representative, it looked as if he could have very little to say as to whether we were to be allowed to proceed or not.

The palaver lasted nearly all day, and as neither party would give in, we parted without having come to any settlement.

Next day they came back again, and once more attempted to induce us to return the way we had come, but finding that was no use, they suggested that we should return by Tashi Lunpo to Rudok, and when I refused to do so, offered to supply transport and food for the whole party free right up to the British frontier; but I told them that if not allowed to go on, I should go straight on to Lhasa and discuss the question there. They were much startled at the idea of our going to the Sacred City, and threatened to oppose us with armed force, saying that they had several thousand men ready to obey their orders. In reply to this I talked big about the merits of breech-loading rifles. It was only a game of brag; neither party meant fighting, and once more they departed leaving things *in statu quo*. The best game to play with them was "masterly inactivity" seasoned with brag, but winter was coming on, and we were dependent on them for provisions, which terribly handicapped us. Before leaving they invited us to dinner the following day, an invitation which we accepted with much pleasure.

Next day, on arriving at their camp, we were ushered in, and being seated on raised carpets, tea was produced; they drank it in Tibetan fashion, mixed with salt and butter, but having found out from our servants the European fashion, they gave us some plain. After a considerable consumption of tea, bowls of mutton, boiled with rice and onions, were brought in; it was really excellent, but eating rice with chopsticks is an art that requires practice. The lower end of the tent was full of the denizens of the neighbouring ones, who walked in and out as if they were members of the great man's family. The whole scene had a very patriarchal air about it. Before

THE CROWD AT THE TENT DOOR.

dining and after the repast, the conversation turned upon the road we were to take, they maintaining that if they allowed us to advance they would be executed on returning to Lhasa, while I stuck to my former statement that I would not go back a yard. Before leaving, I invited them to dine next day with us, and we made our exit amidst much bowing; they were pleasant intelligent men, but exceedingly obstinate. When I pulled the Chinese passport out of my pocket, and asked them what was the meaning of the Amban's presence at Lhasa, if the passport was not to be read or to come into the discussion, they replied that the Amban was allowed to live at Lhasa as a visible sign of the friendship existing between the two countries, but Tibet was in no way under China; at the same time they produced a letter that had been sent after them from Lhasa, in which they were instructed to take no notice of any Chinese passport, but send us back the way we had come.

When they came over the following day to dine with us, they were regaled with tea, curry, etc. After they had eaten their fill, without much circumlocution I offered them a remuneration for any trouble they might be put to or for necessaries supplied, but they said they dared not allow us to go on without an order from Lhasa; but if we gave them a substantial sum and agreed to halt for fifteen days, they would endeavour to procure the necessary permission. To this I agreed, and they departed in order to write a letter to the Deva Zhung. Later, however, they sent a message by one of our men to say that if we agreed to go back eight marches and would give them a thousand rupees, they would allow us to go to China by a road passing to the north of Shiabden Gomba. But they did not say anything about fresh ponies or guides, and as the idea of starting without guides and with exhausted ponies in the month of October on a three months' journey in the wilds was nothing short of madness, I rejected the proposal, telling them if they wanted to gain a thousand rupees, they must do more for it than that.

Next day we went to their tents, and while partaking of boiled mutton and tea they asked many questions about England, and were much surprised to hear that it was surrounded by water, and that people went to it in ships. They had not the faintest idea what a ship was, and asked if it went through the water touching the bottom the whole way. Like true nomads they were particularly curious also about the water and grass.

One of them complained of being ill, and described all sorts of mysterious symptoms he was suffering from. Dr. Thorold gave him a couple of Cockle's pills, on receiving which he asked if, after taking them, he should sleep on his left or his right side. In reply to this question Dr. Thorold gravely told him his right side. To have said it did not matter would never have done.

After the sociable part of the conversation was over, once more the question of our future movements cropped up, and they began to give way a little, and eventually agreed to the following bargain.

We were to go back eight marches, and then travel east by a more northerly route. The Kushok was to accompany us for twelve marches, and after that we should be guided by four men whom he would supply. We were to receive 20 ponies, 2160 lbs. tsampa, 30 sheep, 60 lbs. butter, 1100 lbs. barley, 9 pairs pubboos (Tibetan boots). In return for these I agreed to hand over eight hundred rupees.

This treaty, leaving out all mention of either money or supplies, was drawn up and sealed. The supplies were undoubtedly obtained by requisitions on the inhabitants, which the Kushok did not want the Lhasa authorities to know anything about; but their omission in the written treaty was of no importance, as I would not hand over the rupees before they were received. The guides was a question that gave me more anxiety, as they might lead us into either an impassable country or a nest of Chukpas, and then desert; so I told the Kushok that if they did so, I would certainly march straight on Lhasa and denounce him as a receiver of bribes. He said that there would be no fear of their playing false, as he would clearly explain to them that if they returned without a discharge in writing, they would be punished. The idea of our going back eight marches was in order to allow a report to be made to Lhasa that we had turned back on the road we had come.

As soon as the treaty was concluded, men were sent off in every direction to collect the supplies, and the headman of Shildut, who had been our original jailer, returned to his home. He was a nice old man, and I felt quite sorry at his departure.

The rest of our time at Gagalinchin was principally spent in taking over stores and transport animals. The ponies were sturdy beasts about 12½ hands high, but were all a trifle long in the tooth. However, "never look a gift horse in the mouth," and if they lasted for three months that was all we wanted. The Kushok rather astonished me one day by expressing admiration of our beards, and asking if we had any medicine that would make his grow. As anything like a decent beard is almost unknown in Tibet, I should have thought a hairless face would have been more admired. The Lama was very anxious to know if we had any English poisons. Poisoning is very prevalent in Tibet. If one offers a man tea, he generally refuses it unless some one first drinks some in his presence; and when offering anything to eat or drink, a Tibetan invariably ostentatiously takes some in order to show there is nothing to be afraid of. We were also asked if gold, pearls, and rubies found a place in the European pharmacopœia, and much surprise was expressed when Dr. Thorold assured them that they had no medicinal value. The Talai Lama is regularly dosed with medicines composed of those ingredients, so there is little marvel that all Talai Lamas die young.

4th October, Camp 52; 11 miles.—At last, after a halt of nearly a month at Gagalinchin Camp 51 (15,560), with a temperature varying from 36° to 19°, we were once more marching. During the long halt the weather had been abominable, snow falling off and on all day and night. What fell in the day-time melted at once, but that at night lay till the sun rose and then quickly disappeared. But we were now assured of a spell of fine weather by the Lama, who said he had burnt a herb which was a certain specific against bad weather. He also gave us some charms, consisting of seeds and a miniature model of a human skull made of clay, and said that if ever clouds gathered we had only to throw one into the fire and the sky would at once become clear.

During the eight marches we had agreed to march back, all our things were to be carried on the nomads' animals, in order to ease our own as long as possible. I felt quite appalled at our enormous number of loads, owing to the influx of treaty provisions. The caravan from head to tail was several miles long; the ponies in one squadron heading the procession and seven or eight squadrons at about 600 or 700 yards following in column. Of course a great number of the animals, nine-tenths or so, were carrying the Tibetans' luggage. When one got into camp, it looked as if we should have a long time to wait before getting any tea, as our pots and pans were on a yak some way to the rear, but the Zhung and Kushok Lama very thoughtfully sent us a kettleful. Tibet is a terrible country to travel in as regards distances. An outcrop close to the camp at Gagalinchin appeared about two miles off, but it was a good eleven.

5th October, Toraz Camp 53; 15,660 feet.—An easy march of about 13 miles, crossing a fairly large stream flowing into a lake on the north, to a nomad camp beside some swamps. Black tents were to be seen in almost every direction, and for a nomads' country it was very thickly populated. The inhabitants laugh a great deal, differing very much from the people of India in that respect. A noisier, cheerier lot I have never seen, and one is always inclined to be prepossessed in favour of a light-hearted people. But in the case of the Tibetans a very little knowledge serves to dispel all prepossessions—lying, avaricious, and cowardly; kindness or civility is thrown away on them, and nothing but bullying, or a pretence of bullying, answers.

6th October, Camp 54; Churro, 16 miles.—Overnight the Zhung said he was going to take us by a road going in a more southerly direction, but suspecting it to be a plan to get us on to the Rudok road, I told him that I strongly objected to going so far south, and insisted on being shown another road; he agreed, and we were taken by a road that led rather north of east. For a couple of miles we went along the bank of a swampy lake; the surface was crowded with duck, geese, and teal; where the water was shallow the "*cha toon toon*" (*Grus cinerea*, see page 300), a species of crane, with gray body and black head and tail, was to be seen. Each pair of old birds had a couple of young with them; these young birds, though nearly as big as the parent-birds, differed considerably in plumage, being gray all over.

The Lama went to the edge of the lake and threw

in some valuables, an ancient practice that has at different periods been followed in many countries.

When we got into camp, a tent to serve as kitchen and a small stock of dry fuel were ready for us. The Tibetans evidently meant to be civil, but only one-half of the eight hundred rupees had been paid, which I am afraid had a good deal to do with it. Close to our tents was the nearest approach to a house that we had seen since entering Tibet; it consisted of four stone walls, with a tent made of the usual rough black sacking stretched over in order to serve as roof.

7th October, Camp 55; 16 miles, 15,876 feet.—After crossing an easy pass, we descended into the valley we had travelled down on our way to Gagalinchin. Our Hindustani cook came limping into camp with a most lugubrious expression on his face: according to his story the Tibetans had brought him a pony that had never been mounted before, and as it was his first essay in the equestrian line, he had been thrown, a result that was not to be wondered at.

8th October, Camp 56; 19 miles, 16,400 feet.—Half-way we stopped and had tea with our Tibetan friends and then passing our old camp, No. 48, camped where a fairly large stream, issuing from the snowy mountains on our south, flowed towards the large lake on our north. Another big lake was described to us as lying to the north-west. I made inquiries as to when we were to turn north, and was told just west of Chargat Cho; but the question was where was Chargat Cho? for, amongst other names, nearly every lake we had seen had been called Chargat Cho.

9th October, Camp 57; 11 miles, 15,348 feet.—On the march the large river that had given us a good deal of trouble in fording was recrossed: the water had fallen but was still pretty deep, and a couple of Tibetans on yaks, who were showing the way, came on a deep bit suddenly; yaks and men disappeared under the water, and they only got out again with considerable difficulty, the men presenting a most draggled appearance as they emerged in their wet sheepskins. The appearance of the legs of the Tibetans, who crossed on foot, as they lifted up their garments, wading in, confirmed most strongly the generally accepted idea that they never wash.

After getting into camp, the Zhung sent three ponies, in order to make up the number we were still entitled to by the treaty: they were miserable old patriarchs and I was obliged to refuse to take them, much to the Zhung's chagrin; but the ones he had supplied us with formerly were bad enough, and it was necessary to draw the line somewhere.

10th October.—The Zhung had said the evening before that if we halted for a couple of days there would be no need to go farther west, as he would show us a road running towards the north along the west edge of the lake. I was very glad to get out of the obligation to retrace our steps farther, and the 10th and 11th were spent in interviews and final preparations. He was never tired of asking me to reiterate my promise of avoiding Shiabden Gomba. I always did so with the reservation that, if the guides played false in any way, I should march straight on Lhasa *viâ* Shiabden Gomba, or any other place. This always called forth loud protestations of the utter impossibility of there being any chance of the faithful guides provided playing false in any way, or leaving us without first obtaining our permission.

The tales Tibetans tell, and I really think believe in, are sometimes most marvellous. We were told of a country not far off where men lived who possessed only one arm and one leg, but no one would allow that he had seen any of these interesting people, and they would not even say in which direction the country lay. Another wonderful country was one on the road to China, where the people had pigs' heads, but, as with the other one, no one present had ever been there or seen the inhabitants, though nearly everybody knew some one else who had. Another story we were told was about a lake away to the north called Tso Ngom Mo, or the blue lake—so large that it took thirty-five days to ride round. Formerly no lake existed, but some Changpas lifted up a large flat stone and water immediately gushed out and submerged the country. An animal is found in the lake and nowhere else whose skin is of fabulous value. Once a year one has to be sent to the Emperor of China. Should it be omitted by any chance, several dignitaries would lose their heads, but no one seemed very clear about who were the dignitaries who were to be thus summarily punished for neglect of duty towards the sun of Heaven. The lake meant must have been Koko Nor, but it is terribly hard work trying to get geographical information out of Tibetans, and when in exceptional cases, as does occasionally happen, a vein of truth runs through their statements, it is so fine as to be almost impossible to discover.

I was much struck with the respect shown by the nomads to those in authority over them: taking off their hats and continually sticking out their tongues and bowing whenever spoken to.

The air in these regions seems much charged with electricity. On stroking a dog, sparks are given out with a crackling sound; the same thing happens often with cats in other parts of the world, but I have never before known it happen in the case of dogs.

October 12th, Camp 58; 9 miles, 15,500 feet.—A pleasant easy march up the western edge of the lake. From camp a beautiful view down the lake was obtained, with an island in the foreground, called, in memory of some great legendary warrior, Spamo's Helmet. Near where the rivers enter on the south-west side, the water had quite a greenish colour, but towards the other end it was bright blue.

Dr. Thorold operated with much success with an ordinary pair of pincers on a Tibetan suffering from toothache.

October 13th, Camp 59; 15,500 feet.—Soon

after leaving the last camp we crossed a small pass on the top of which was a heap of stones ornamented with bright rags stuck on sticks.[1] The Tibetans who had brought animals to assist our transport were anxious to return, but I refused to allow any one to go until the full number of ponies promised had been supplied, and as yet none had been given in place of those rejected.

October 14th, Camp 60; 20 miles, 15,463 feet.—We were very late starting, as most of the morning was taken up in endeavouring to exchange two of our old worn-out ponies for two good-conditioned ones. Tibetans are pretty wide-awake in anything of the nature of a bargain, and knowing well that we could not halt long enough to get our animals into condition, and that it was absolutely necessary for us to have animals fit to start on a long journey, they held out most obstinately.

Eventually I had to give an additional sixty rupees, which I suppose was quite as much as their ponies were worth according to ordinary rates.

The route lay across a wide valley, in which were undulating hills scattered about: the direction had too much west in it to please me, so I remonstrated with the Zhung, and was told that next day we would go in a more easterly direction. The camp was in a very exposed windy spot near a spring lying east of a large lake. Five marches in a north-west direction lay the country of Tung Chang, whose inhabitants

[1] See page 146.

owed allegiance neither to Lhasa nor China. The same may be said of many of the nomad tribes living in outlying parts.

October 15th, Camp 61; 12 miles, 15,538 feet.—On getting up in the morning it was found that in the night one of our two surviving donkeys had been eaten by wolves:—poor brute, he had done right good service, and I was extremely sorry to hear of his tragic end.

The route still lay across the valley, and the snowy range on the north still appeared to be nearly as far off as ever. When first sighted, it had appeared only about ten miles away, and after two days' marching it still seemed nearly the same distance off. After we got into camp, the Kushok Lama, who had previously told us that, according to the rules of his order, it would be better to die than touch wine, sent over to ask if we could let him have a little to be taken as medicine, as he was not feeling well. Many is the time I have heard the same yarn from natives of India. I got both the Zhung and Kushok Lama to come over to our tent, and told them that I thought it would be a pity to take them farther out of their way, and that we could very easily go on now with the guides only. They agreed to go back, but said we could not possibly part without first halting and feasting together for a couple of days. I demurred a good deal to this, as winter was coming on and we had a long journey in front of us, but eventually agreed to halt for one day. In the morning we breakfasted with the Zhung; he gave us plates of minced meat and rice, followed by rice mixed with ghi (clarified butter) and gur (molasses); the first was excellent, but in spite of our Tibetan appetites we shied a little at the latter.

In reply to our inquiries, he said that the reason of the friendship that existed between China and Tibet was that many years ago there were three brothers who were Lamas of great sanctity; one took the Buddhist religion into China, one into Tibet, and the third was a wanderer. Ever since that time the two countries had been closely allied—a story that hardly agrees with accepted history according to which the Buddhist religion was introduced several centuries prior to Lamaism, which was an innovation of the eighth century. The conversation then turned on the subject of Chukpas, who mostly come from Kamba Golok: he said that the Deva Zhung was making great efforts to stamp them out, and that orders had been issued to catch and execute them whenever it was possible to do so. The mode of execution was first of all to sew them up in leather and expose them to a hot sun for some time; after that they were thrown into a river or lake.

He then harked back to the old subject of Shiabden Gomba, repeating his former statement that to a certainty he would lose his life if we went there. I told him again, as I had told him fifty times before, that if the guides played fair he might rely upon it that we would not go. After that I gave him two hundred rupees, the last instalment of the promised money, and some cloth, a revolver, and other articles, and in return he gave me some brick tea, butter, rice, gur, and a little rat of a pony: these things were given amidst many protestations that he felt ashamed at receiving such valuable gifts from a guest and a stranger and giving such poor ones in return. This fine speech, however, did not prevent him asking for some coral beads to take home to his two daughters. Later in the evening, when we were back in our tents, he sent a man to ask for them, and a message by one of our men requesting that they might be made up into a package and sealed to prevent the messenger stealing any on the road.

How these Tibetans trust one another!

After leaving his tent we went to the Kushok Lama's, where we had a repast of much the same nature, with the addition of some little biscuit-like cakes, which he assured us he had made with his own hands; they were really excellent. I presented him with two hundred rupees, some yellow broadcloth, a galvanic battery, and a watch, receiving in return a lot of butter, some brick tea, some fine flour, a piece of very inferior English cloth, a cup with a silver saucer and cover, some tsampa, and a pony of nominal value. We also all received scarves of greeting: those given to Dr. Thorold and myself were made of fine Chinese silk, which the Lama himself put round our necks, while

TIBETAN CUP AND SPOON.

those given to our followers were most shoddy arrangements. We both mutually gave small sums also to each other's servants. In spite of his priestly office he had set his heart on getting a revolver, and begged hard for one, but as we only had two in the party and might want them, I declined: he had not breeding enough to hide the pique he felt at my refusal. However, he soon got over his fit of the sulks, and having been unsuccessful in his efforts to get a revolver, he started begging that I would give him my spring-balance weighing-machine. As Dr. Thorold also had one, and one between us was quite enough, I agreed and gave it to him. Tibetans are not a people who will ever lack anything for want of asking.

In the evening both the Zhung and Kushok came over to our tents, and we feasted them. Afterwards the guides were sent for, and got their orders in our presence. They were to guide us to Tarsedo (Ta Chen lu), and on no account to leave us without first having obtained a formal discharge in writing. Should they do so, on returning to their homes they would be punished. They agreed to it, and giving me their hands, swore to be faithful.

17th October, Camp 62; 10 miles, 16,238 feet.—We rose early, and after loading up, went first of all to the Lama Kushok's tent to say good-bye. On entering we were seated on carpets, and had a little desultory conversation, in which he announced his intention of visiting India, and hoped he would meet us there. We parted with many protestations of regret, which were just as sincere on one side as another, and loud protestations from him of his intention of praying regularly for us. We then went over to the Zhung's tent; he started again the well-worn subject of Shiabden Gomba, and got once more the stereotyped answer. He seemed interested in commerce, and told us that he had sent a hundred horse-loads of wool to Darjiling, and had made a large profit on it, quite forgetting that not long before, when the subject of which way we were to go was on the tapis, and the name of Darjiling was mentioned, he had utterly denied all knowledge of such a place; now it appeared he had regular commercial dealings with it. In addition to wool, he had a hundred musk pods and a thousand yaks' tails ready to send if ruling rates were likely to be favourable. He wanted me to assist him, but not being in the yak-tail-musk-pod business myself, I did not see my way to it; as, however, he insisted on getting a letter, thinking it might be useful if he visited India, I gave him one. The love of chits[1]—the passion that in the Indian servant's bosom strives for mastery with the potent love of pice—is evidently not unknown in upper circles in Tibet. We parted from him with the same loud protestations of sorrow that marked our parting from the Kushok Lama, but, as became their different offices, the bye-allusions in one case were to prayer and in the other to business.

[1] A chit is a written testimonial.

CHAPTER VII

MARCHING NORTHWARDS

18th October, Camp 63; 14 miles, 16,668 feet.—At last we managed to get over the snowy range that had been staring us in the face for several days. The pass was 18,768 feet high; there was not much snow on it, but the wind was bitterly cold, and we did not linger on the top. After descending, the Tibetan yak-drivers wanted to halt at a place where there was very little grass and no water, but I absolutely refused to do so, and insisted on their coming on until we got to water. A few miles farther on we found a spring and camped. I then let them all go with a small gratuity, which much astonished and delighted them, the Tibetan custom being to exact transport and pay nothing. We were now dependent on our own animals for carriage,—the tow-rope being fairly cast off and an uninhabited country in front, I sincerely hoped there were not going to be many high passes to be crossed, as nothing takes it out of horseflesh so much as struggling over these under heavy loads. Tibetan antelope were once more to be seen.

19th October, Camp 64; 10 miles, 16,363 feet.—We were rather a long time getting off; as some of the ponies we had got from the Changpas were evidently unused to loads, loading them was a matter of considerable difficulty, and they kicked and plunged, occasionally breaking away, and were only re-caught with considerable difficulty. At last we started, and travelled down the bed of a stream that flowed roughly in a north-west direction, but wound about considerably; it had to be crossed and recrossed several times, which was a work of considerable difficulty, as, though it was coated with ice, the ice was just not strong enough to bear laden ponies. The wind all day blowing from west-south-west was extremely cold, and as the sun was obscured by heavy snow clouds it froze steadily, and the water on the dogs and the horses' legs congealed directly they emerged from the water.

Of the four Tibetan guides only one seemed to have any idea of the road, and that a rather hazy one, but they were willing enough to work, and lent a hand in loading the animals and driving them.

On the road several herds of burhel were seen and some horns of *Ovis ammon*.

20th October, Camp 65; 12 miles, 15,760 feet.—A bitterly cold morning when we rose and struck camp, but just as we started the sun came out brightly, and we thought we should have a fine day; later on, however, clouds came up and snow fell on the surrounding hills, but we were fortunate enough to escape it. The stream we had been following disappeared in the soil, a habit Tibetan streams have got, but we managed to find a spring of fresh water. One of the guides told us that we should reach a place before long where bears were plentiful, and that on the road *nyan* (*Ovis ammon*) abounded; but I think he was wrong. I doubt *Ovis ammon* abounding anywhere; that they are found scattered over a very wide stretch of country is undoubted, but, unlike yak and antelope, nowhere did we find them very common.

On getting up next morning it was found that some of our ponies had strayed in the night, and as they were not recovered before the afternoon, we were obliged to halt for the day.

22nd October, Camp 66; 13 miles, 16,263 feet.—A pony was missing in the morning, but as he was a real gift horse, having been presented by the Zhung, and far and away the worst in the caravan, I decided to march, leaving two men to search in the valleys close by, with orders to come on after the caravan quickly whether they found him or not.

The Hindustani cook was a great trouble, as, although he was knocking up simply through never walking, yet when not given a pony to ride he lay down on the ground and would not move. It was hard to know what to do with him; if left behind he would assuredly have perished directly the sun went down; whilst riding, he arrived in camp every day quite numbed with cold. He had got into an apathetic state, and was perfectly indifferent whether he lived or died.

In the afternoon the two men whôm I had left behind rejoined us, having failed to find the missing pony.

23rd October, Camp 67; 13 miles, 16,563 feet.—The road still lay in a northerly direction, and crossing a small *col* we found ourselves in a wide open valley, with small lakes scattered about, and herds of kiang, goa, and antelope grazing in every direction. A mule knocked up on the road and had to be shot.

The Hindustani cook managed to lag behind sufficiently to allow the caravan to get out of sight, and then lost his way. Men had to be sent out to look for him, and eventually he was brought in.

At camp when we arrived there was some water, but within an hour of sunset it was frozen solid, and not a drop to be got for love or money; the water question with winter coming on was assuming a more acute phase, as finding fresh water had always been a matter of difficulty, and now the difficulty was increased by the probability of finding it frozen. Sufficient fuel could generally be found to thaw enough for our own wants, but it was quite impossible to thaw enough for the animals. I told the guides that I had had quite enough marching north, and was now determined to go east. They promised that after doing one more march in the direction we were going, we should turn due east.

24th October, Camp 68; 14 miles, 15,863 feet.—Still going in a very northerly direction, with a snowy range lying to the east of us. Towards evening we came to a watercourse in which there was a little water, mostly frozen, fed by a spring, beside which we pitched our camp. Round the spring there were some traps set for antelope, consisting of a ring of about eight inches diameter, in which were sharp pegs made of horn converging downwards; the animal, if he put his foot through, would be unable to extricate it, and as the ring was secured to a buried horn, could not get away with it.

AN ANTELOPE TRAP.

One of the guides told some of the caravan drivers that the caravanbashi had received a bribe from the Tibetans to take us as far north as possible, and had lied regarding several matters. I sent for him (the guide) to my tent, and questioned him; he had little to say against the caravanbashi, but he admitted that there was a road going more easterly than the one we were taking, so I told him that if he would take us to Tarsedo (Ta Chen Lu) by a road running either south of or through Chiamdo, he would be well rewarded;

but if he attempted to take us any farther north, I would simply steer my own course, and most probably go through Shiabden Gomba. He said if we did that he would certainly lose his head; to which I replied, "Well, then, it is in your own hands; take us in an easterly direction just avoiding Shiabden Gomba, and you will be well rewarded, but farther north I will not go." He promised faithfully that he would do so.

25th October, Camp 69; 24 miles, 16,663 feet.—As we started, I found to my astonishment that the guide did not intend to act as agreed on the previous evening, was guiding us north-east, and utterly denying all that he had told me. I absolutely refused to go in that direction, and the whole four of them solemnly protested that there was no other road. I said, "All right, I shall show you the road to Shiabden Gomba," and altering the direction I steered straight for a depression in the mountains in a south-easterly direction. They followed, clamouring that they would lose their heads if we went any farther in that direction, and falling down on their knees seized my hands, but still obstinately maintained that there was no road due east, while I exhorted them to show on one, saying that I had come much farther north than was in the contract, and was not going another yard in that direction. If there was no road east, then the only thing to do was to go to Shiabden Gomba. For a long time they maintained there was no such road; but at last they gave in, acknowledged there was, and the direction being changed we headed east under their guidance, passing a herd of at least sixty wild yaks. I should much have liked to bag one, as their skin is excellent for repairing boots, but they were on a piece of very open ground where stalking was out of the question, so they were allowed to rest in peace. In the afternoon no signs of water were to be seen, and not much snow. One of the guides who had gone on in front to search, had not returned, and I began to fear he had bolted, especially as another was missing, and a third had been caught attempting to desert. I sent forward a man on a pony to search both for water and the missing man, but he returned reporting no signs of either. This looked very much as if we should have to go thirsty to bed that night, when on topping a ridge, to our great joy, the guide was discovered beside a frozen pool of water in the bed of a stream, where, by breaking the ice a little, water was got, but not enough to thoroughly satisfy the ponies.

26th October, Camp 70; 12 miles, 16,538 feet.—A bitterly cold day. As we ascended a pass, clouds were scudding up from the west, and on the top of the pass the fine dry snow was being driven hither and thither by the wind. From the top of the pass we descended by a narrow stony valley, in which a herd of burhel were grazing, into a broad open one with a lake in it. In one place the stream, descending from the pass for about twenty yards, was quite clear of ice, so the ponies were able to drink their fill

—a thing they had not done for several days. The wind was so strong that getting the tents up was a work of considerable difficulty, and in addition it was so cold that it was almost impossible to touch the iron pegs; if one did, one's hands became so numbed that it was a considerable time before they were of any use. Driving the pegs into the frozen ground was also a matter of great delicacy, as they broke on the least provocation.

The missing guide rejoined in the afternoon, but we never found out where he had been or where he had spent the night.

27th October, Camp, 71; 6 miles, 16,838 feet.—On getting up in the morning it was found that one pony had been frozen to death in the night, and several more were missing. It was eleven o'clock before the missing ones were found, and twelve before we started, so we only managed to make a very small march. From a ridge that we ascended, a lake was seen in front. The guides wanted us to go to the north of it, as they said all the land to the south was in the district of Namru, which we were not to enter; but as I had told them before that our course was going to be east as much as possible, and when an inclination to either side had to be made, south was to be taken in preference to north, I declined, and a line was maintained that would take us just south of it.

There was a good deal of grass near our camp, and as I was rather seedy, we halted for a couple of days.

HEAD OF *OVIS AMMON.*

30th October, Camp 72; 15 miles, 16,763 feet.—Circling round the south of the lake which was intensely salt, and then over a ridge, we found ourselves in an open valley.

31st October, Camp 73; 15 miles, 16,263 feet.—At the head of the valley in which our last camp had been a small pass was crossed, and a country much cut up by nullahs was entered; in one of these we camped by a frozen stream. Smashing the ice to look for water was rather a difficult business, as our only axe was broken, and it had to be done with stones. Under the ice a little water slowly trickled forth, and it was a long time before all the horses were satisfied. One of the guides said he had once been three months in this place on the watch to give notice of any parties of Chukpas who might pass along, coming from Kamba Golok; during that time he saw many bears, but now they seemed to be all hibernating, for we never saw any.

1st November, Camp 74; 18 miles, 16,463 feet.—From this camp a very well worn path, rising almost to the dignity of a road, ran in a north-west direction; the guides said it went to Tuman Chaka, a lake two marches distant, whence salt was obtained for the Lhasa market. I tried to find out from the guides when we were likely to commence descending, as the cold was telling terribly on the animals, but they were very sketchy in their knowledge of the country, every one of them giving a different answer. Our sole remaining donkey was a most depressing-looking animal as he marched along, the effect of his naturally somewhat mournful expression being heightened by the huge icicles below each eye, formed from frozen tears.

2nd November, Camp 75; 19 miles, 16,363 feet.—Close to the camp there were some human bones, the remains of two Chukpas who had been killed the year before by a party of Tibetans. One of the guides told me a story of how the people of Kamba Golok at one time were good faithful subjects of the Deva Zhung, but they threw off all allegiance, and took to robbing their neighbours. An army from Lhasa invaded their country; this frightened them, and they sent a deputation to wait on the general, and, pleading poverty, asked for permission to do one grand loot, promising after that to return to their allegiance and live quietly. The leave was granted, and ever since they have been robbing steadily, utterly refusing to carry out their part of the contract. They are not nearly so well armed as the ordinary Tibetan nomads, having, according to the guide, who had a very poor idea of their valour, only a sword and matchlock to every three or four men, whereas, amongst the peaceful population, every man is armed. Much impressed by the effect on antelope and yak produced by breech-loading rifles, the guides suggested that, in the event of our meeting a party of Chukpas laden with plunder, it would be both pleasant and profitable to attack them.

The march was a long cold one; heavy clouds

coming up from the south-west obscured the sun, and when the sun is not visible at these altitudes, life becomes a burden. One pony was utterly unable to keep up with the caravan, so I had him shot, the most merciful thing that could be done under the circumstances. There were enormous numbers of yak about, and the Tibetans, galloping after a herd, succeeded in singling one out and riding it down; it was a half-grown bull, and appeared to me very like an escaped tame one that had joined his wild brethren, but I have no doubt that on good ground a veritable wild one could easily be ridden to a standstill.

3rd November, Camp 76; 26 miles, 16,113 feet.—A long march over undulating hills. We started with a cloudless sky, but before long clouds came up and snow fell. I sent a Tibetan ahead to keep a look-out for water, but he did not find any till late in the afternoon, when about 3 miles north of our line a frozen stream was discovered, whose course was towards a lake on the north-west; under the ice a little water was found, but not nearly enough. The animals were having a very bad time—intense cold, hard work, scanty grass, and a little water once a day; their knocking-up was not to be wondered at. Our reaching an inhabited country before they all succumbed was getting doubtful. Dr. Thorold and myself were much annoyed by the irritable state our skin had got into, and put it down to the intense dryness of the atmosphere, but subsequently it struck us that the irritability had been unknown previous to the advent of the Tibetan guides; reasoning on this basis, the cure was promptly discovered—insect powder, an article that previous experience had led me to consider absolutely indispensable in Asiatic travel. The guides now united in saying that in four days we should begin to descend, but whether they knew or not was doubtful; and, in any case, they were such liars that it was impossible to believe anything they said.

4th November, Camp 77; 11 miles, 16,238 feet.—After the march the Tibetans made out that we would have to do another five marches before beginning to descend.

5th November, Camp 78; 11 miles, 16,148 feet.—About 5 miles of the march lay along a road that comes from Tuman Chaka; after leaving it we went about 6 miles to a place where there was a pool of water not quite frozen to the bottom, and camped.

6th November, Camp 79; 13 miles, 16,139 feet.—After leaving the last camp we ascended a small and easy pass, and descended into a wide open valley in which some yak were grazing. To the north-east a range of mountains with some fine snowy peaks, evidently the Dang La range, was seen, and in the valley a stream was flowing in an east-south-east direction.

7th November, Camp 80; 14 miles, 15,689 feet.—A slight descent all the way. Every one much exercised in their minds as to whether we were at last to commence descending from the great Tibetan plateau.

8th November, Camp 81; 10 miles, 15,439 feet.—The first part of the march was down the bed of the same stream, the Sang Po, and then crossing on the ice (a difficult operation, as it was very slippery, and sand had to be plentifully sprinkled on the surface before the animals could get over), we ascended a pass. The hills were of a sandy nature with numbers of springs, and coarse grass was plentiful. When we camped I decided to halt for a day in order to give the animals a rest.

The ravens in these high regions are a great puzzle; here numbers were always round our camp, and in the most sterile parts of the Chang, if any animal was being cut up, a few always appeared to claim their share; what they lived on was the marvel. They are a quarrelsome ill-natured lot; when two are gathered together a fight is always sure to be going on. A lammergeir was circling round the camp most of the day. They are birds that, though plentiful nearly all over the Himalayas, avoid the very high plateau of Central Tibet.

As water was abundant, I washed—an eccentricity on my part that absolutely horrified the camp-followers.

A thermometer stuck in a sheltered corner with the sun shining on it went up to +66°, but in the night it went down to –14°, being a range of 80°.

10th November, Camp 82; 15,194 feet.—In the

night, wolves got at the sheep and killed seven; several more were so badly mauled that they had to be slaughtered. The brutes managed to commit their depredation without disturbing any one in the camp.

In the afternoon I put the guides through a long cross-examination, the result being to leave me in as great doubt as ever as to whether they were absolutely ignorant or not of all knowledge of the country.

11th November, Camp 83; 19 miles, 15,389 feet.—After crossing a small ridge, we came to a largish stream, about 80 yards wide; we had to follow it up a little distance before finding a place to cross, where it was completely frozen over. The guides called it the Sang Po; the same name they had given to the stream we had crossed two days previously, though obviously the two could not be the same. After crossing it, some men were seen in the distance; they circled round and then advanced to meet us; they turned out to be a party of Chukpas on a marauding expedition; every man carried matchlock, sword, and a very long spear—as unprepossessing-looking a lot of ruffians as any one could wish to meet. They began abusing the guides for bringing strangers into the country, but I put a stop to that and we rode on. They were mounted on very good sturdy little ponies, and two additional ones carried the baggage of the party.

While we were pitching our tents, two more men

were seen in the distance and shortly afterwards one of them rode into the camp ; he described himself as a Nakchu man, and said he had come to this place to hunt yak. The district he called Bongro, and the river we had crossed, which was the boundary of the Deva Zhung's territory, he called Chang Sakia Sang Po.

He said the Chukpas did not as a rule commit robberies so far east, but it would be as well to keep a look-out during the night, as after we had parted from them he had noticed that they had circled round and were now somewhere in the neighbouring hills watching our camp. I sent out a patrol, who returned having seen nothing, but a sentry for the night was posted, as it is always well to be on the safe side, though the probabilities of their attacking were not great.

12th November, Camp 84; 13 miles, 15,469 feet.—The country round about, though 1000 feet lower, is of much the same character as the Chang, the rivers flowing in any and every direction. The tracks of a bear were most distinctly seen, but they were very old. Wolves kept prowling about the camp, very insolent but very wary; it was almost impossible ever to get a shot at one.

13th November, Camp 85; 17 miles, 15,694 feet.—Here we found ourselves in an inhabited country. Nomads' black tents were scattered about the valleys, and on the hill-sides herds and flocks were grazing. The district, which is called Amdo, is said to hold two hundred tents. Zama is four days distant in a north-easterly direction, the Dang La Pass was six days, and Shiabden south-south-east three days. Ta Chen Lu was said to be five months, an obvious exaggeration; it could not well be more than two and a half.

14th November, Camp 86; 15 miles, 15,439 feet.—After proceeding for a mile or two we came to a tent, where we stopped to ask the way. The good man was out, but his wife sent her son, a boy of about twelve, to show the road; he took us over a pass, then down to a river called the Thoga Long Pa Chu, which was a mass of rotten and half-rotten ice, and gave us some difficulty crossing; then over another pass called the Buntsu La, and down by a narrow ravine into a wide valley; towards the west end of which was a lake called Chonak Cho; several tents were to be seen scattered about. Our youthful guide deserted somewhere in the intricacies of the ravine. It snowed off and on all day—a most serious matter for the ponies—as with snow on the ground it was almost impossible for them to pick up a living.

PERDIX SIFANICA (see page 300).

CHAPTER VIII

ENTERING INHABITED COUNTRY

15th November, Camp 87; 15 miles, 14,890 feet.—In the night the clouds passed away; and as we started the sun was getting up in a clear blue sky. I sent a man over to some neighbouring tents to try and procure transport animals. He rejoined us on the march, bringing the headman with him. We had a great palaver, the upshot of which was that he would supply us with guides and yak as far as the frontier of Chinese Tibet, which was two marches distant, but he could not get the animals all at once, so it was necessary that we should halt a couple of days to give him time to collect them. This was a red-letter day with us for two reasons—firstly, we were below 15,000 feet, and secondly, we had now arrived in a country where transport was procurable, and we no longer were dependent on our own exhausted animals. Next day about midday the headman turned up, bringing the promised transport. He said that the year before two Europeans, evidently M. Bonvalôt and Prince Henri of Orleans, had come from the north over the Dang La Pass, and thence had entered Namru, where they had been stopped.

17th November, Camp 88; 19 miles, 14,740 feet.—Up a valley with innumerable springs and boggy ground, which fortunately was all frozen. The men said they saw a bear, but I was ahead of the caravan at the time and did not see it. A mule unable to keep up had to be abandoned.

18th November, Camp 89; 17 miles, 14,925 feet.—Before starting, some men were discovered in a valley close by. I sent a caravan driver to find out who they were, and obtain as much information about the roads, etc., as he could. He returned saying they were a party of merchants from Ta Chen Lu, bringing tea and tobacco. Samples of both were produced; the tea was utter rubbish, and as for the tobacco neither in appearance nor flavour did it bear any resemblance whatever to the fragrant leaf, but seemed to be made out of a sort of touchwood. They said there were two roads to Ta Chen Lu; they had come by the easier, and had been two months and eleven days over it.

For some days we had been marching over a country with bright red rocks and soil, but now we entered a typical granitic country; huge boulders were lying about, and here and there were large patches of boggy ground with tussocky grass; there was a great deal of it about the place we camped in, and as it takes much snow to quite cover it, such places are utilised by the nomads as winter quarters.

Near us there was a large camp of them. They build a wall of argols round the west sides of the tents as a protection against the prevailing wind, and make sheep-pens of the same material. Outside each tent several large stacks of it were to be seen. I sent over to call the headman and ask for transport; in reply a youth came, who said that the headman lived half a day's march distant, and without an order from him nothing could be done, but he would find out and bring an answer before morning. I asked him if this country was under China or Lhasa; he said that we were now in Chinese territory, and that the inhabitants were in no way under the Deva Zhung.

The sun was losing much of its power, and even in the day-time tea poured into a cup froze very quickly.

19th November, Camp 90.—As in the evening I had discovered that it was all a fabrication about the headman living half a day's march distant, but that in reality he only lived a mile off, when day broke we moved over and, pitching our camp beside his, sent a man to call him; a youth, who turned out to be his son, came over, but I feigned anger at the big man's not coming himself, and refused to treat with the youth. He departed much cowed, and the headman himself quickly appeared. After being seated in my tent he asked to see the passport, and when it was produced became quite friendly, and promised transport and guides to the next headman's tents. He could not read a word; therefore an old newspaper or bill would equally well have passed muster. I tried to make an arrangement with him for transport and guides as far as Ta Chen Lu, but although I offered good pay he would have nothing to say to it, though he said he would be glad enough to supply carriage free as far as his district went, and that all the way to Ta Chen Lu the headmen, of whom there were thirty-nine, would do the same. The fact was that he was rather shy of getting into trouble for having dealings with strangers, but at the same time was anxious to see us out of his domains. After a pretty long sojourn in the East I don't hesitate to rank the Tibetans as liars above all people I have met. From about a dozen men I asked the name of this place, and received a different answer in each case. The right name I am inclined to think is Atak Thomar, as that was what it was called by people two stages back.

20th November, Camp 91; 15 miles, 14,900 feet.—The promised yaks did not turn up until about 9 A.M., which involved rather a late start. The going all day was exceedingly bad, as the whole country was covered, almost to the summits of the hills, with tussocky grass, with a hole round each tussock about a foot deep.

The four Deva Zhung's men were very anxious to leave us, as they said the Giate (Chinese subjects) had threatened to cut off their heads for bringing Europeans into the country, but I refused to let them go, as their presence in the camp was a proof that things had been amicably arranged with the Lhasa authorities; and besides the bond was that they were to be discharged on our reaching Ta Chen Lu and not before.

In the night our only minimum thermometer was broken by a yak. It was a great loss, and the only way left to ascertain how low the thermometer went was to look at an ordinary one just before sunrise every morning.

21st November, Camp 92; 16 miles, 14,525 feet. —Crossing a small pass, and descending the bed of a stream, we reached the headquarters of another nomads' district. The pansang, or headman, came over to see us, and promised to make all arrangements for carriage on. After returning to his tent he sent a present of a pailful of milk, which was very acceptable both as an unwonted luxury and as a proof of his good-will. According to him there were two roads to Ta Chen Lu; one, the more northerly, went by Gyakundo, and the other through Chiamdo and Bathang. At Ta Chen Lu there were European merchants and missionaries, who had built houses with glass windows.

22nd November, Camp 93; 9 miles, 14,325 feet. —In the morning the pansang turned up, bringing six yaks, and apologising for the delay in bringing the rest, as they were grazing at a place some distance off. As I suspected, it was only a plan to delay us. We loaded the six yaks, and left some grain and tsampa in charge of a couple of men to be brought on afterwards. There was one thing in the pansang's favour: he was the only Tibetan who had given information flavoured with a probability of containing a certain amount of truth.

The method employed to reduce an intractable yak to submission was for two men to each seize a horn and jerk outwards with all the strength they could muster; every jerk it looked as if the horns would part from their sockets, but no such calamity happened, and on being released the animal was quite cowed, and stood perfectly still to allow himself to be loaded.

About two miles after starting we crossed a well-worn road, which runs from Lhasa to Sining, with a branch going over the Dang La pass. The country was fairly thickly populated, and, so far as we had seen in Chinese Tibet, the population was thicker than in independent Tibet. But of course the reason was that since leaving the Deva Zhung's frontier we had been gradually descending, and consequently the country had been becoming more habitable. The things left behind were brought on in the afternoon with a message from the pansang that if we had any difficulties about getting yaks we should seize them and beat the people if they objected. What is known in India as *zubburdusti* is evidently not unknown in Tibet.

The headman of the place we had arrived at paid us a visit, presenting, in addition to the inevitable khatag, or scarf of greeting, some milk. He promised to supply yaks in the morning. As I had heard that there were many thieves about, I impressed upon him that he would be held responsible for anything stolen. He did not like the idea, but seemed to look upon it as just.

A grateful patient who had been physicked by Dr. Thorold presented some butter of really excellent quality, a great treat after the rancid filth we had been accustomed to.

23rd November, Camp 94; 19 miles, 14,200 feet.—The promised yaks turned up before daylight, so there was no need to put into execution the pansang of Memar Atak's advice about beating the principal inhabitants. The road ran over peaty ground most of the way, and then down to a river that was only just fordable. When the snows are melting it must be quite impassable. Another pony gave up and had to be shot; it was becoming a regular routine practice having to shoot one, and sometimes more, every day. On the road some wolf-traps were passed. They consist of a hollow dug out under the ground. The mouth is closed by a board, which if pressed upon gives way, thus releasing a stone which tightens a noose placed round the neck of the hole.

Wolves are a regular scourge in these parts, committing great depredations amongst the flocks, the sole wealth of the people.

The way the camp-followers proceeded on the Asiatic motto of "Never do your work if you can get somebody else to do it," was strikingly exemplified. Loading up, striking tents, collecting fuel, or whatever else was to be done, they invariably managed to induce some Tibetan who had come to gaze at the stranger to assist,—a plan that had my heartiest support as discouraging curiosity and accelerating work.

24th November, Camp 95; 10 miles, 14,025 feet. —The four Tibetans supplied by the Lhasa people were clamouring to be allowed to return, saying they were certain to have their heads cut off by Chinese subjects if they went on any farther; but I had heard too much about the decapitation business. It had become a cry of wolf, and had ceased to be impressive, so they were told it was in the bond that they were to go to Ta Chen Lu, and to Ta Chen Lu they would have to go.

Having assembled all the principal inhabitants, I tried to get some information out of them about the road and country, but it was no use. They professed ignorance and told lies, leaving me as wise as ever, but they promised to supply carriage on in the morning, which was a matter of much more moment than obtaining the information.

However, later in the evening it was discovered that, owing to my having spoken civilly to them—a great mistake dealing with either Chinese or Tibetans —they had got a bit above themselves, and had been telling the men that had come with us, "You brought these foreigners into the country; you can take them where you like, but they will get no help from us." I at once summoned them and spoke to them, taking particular care to avoid my former error of too much politeness. The result was that the yaks and ponies previously promised were brought in within a couple of hours. It is a long time before one thoroughly understands what a mistake it is ever to be polite, or assume any affectation of friendliness, with Tibetans or Chinese. Even after being taught by experience the folly of it, I have unconsciously often treated them with courtesy and consideration, only to find in return that, while possibly showing politeness outwardly, they would lay themselves out to covertly degrade one in the eyes of the people by insults so far-fetched as often to be quite unperceived at the time, and would invariably manage to shuffle out of any compact. By taking a high tone, civility, and as much honesty as their natures are capable of, are insured.

25th November, Camp 96; 15 miles, 14,025 feet.—We rose very early intending to make a long march, but much sooner than we expected arrived at Nakchu Satuk, where the big man, who was to give us transport, resided. As soon as tents were pitched, I sent a caravan driver to call him; in response a man came over, and, apologising for the great man's absence, said he was acting for him, and would be happy to do anything we wanted. I asked for carriage and guides, to which he replied that the men who had brought us, according to the custom of the country, should take us a few miles farther on, and that from that place he would be responsible; and that if we went there in the morning he would have everything ready, so that we could change the loads from one lot of animals on to another, and there would be no delay. I agreed to this, exhorting him not to fail in his promise, and he departed, protesting that if we did not find the animals waiting for us we would be at liberty to cut off his head. But, alas, he protested too much!

Two Tibetans came riding past the camp. I told one of the men to call them, but they rode off as hard as their ponies could go. The fear of strangers seems universal in these parts, and is not only extended to foreigners, but all Tibetans seem frightened of each other.

26th November, Camp 97; 7 miles, 14,450 feet.—Got up in the morning before dawn, wishing to make an early start, and proceeded to awake the camp. It was bitterly cold, and several inches of snow lay on the ground, so it is not to be wondered at that no one showed any feverish haste in responding to the call. The Hindustani cook comfortably in bed called out from the inside of a tent that he was up and getting things ready; half-an-hour afterwards, hearing nothing, I looked in and found he had gone off to sleep again. I thoroughly awoke him that time.

We started just as the sun was getting up, but the combination of snow and tussocky grass was very bad going, and it was midday before we reached the place where we were to be met by the relief of baggage animals; but on arrival there, instead of seeing the animals, we found our loudly-protesting friend with a squad of women clearing the snow away from a place for us to pitch our tents in. When I asked about the yaks, he said that there were two other headmen in the place, and as yet they had not sent their quota, but they would arrive soon, and in the meanwhile we had better halt for the day; though much annoyed, there was nothing to do but acquiesce. At least a thousand yaks were to be seen, but he said they were all milk ones, and in confirmation thereof gave us a pailful of milk; he also was good enough to give us a couple of sacks of dry argols. With the ground covered with snow it would have been impossible to get any for ourselves, so we felt duly grateful for his thoughtfulness. During the day the snow showed no signs of melting; there is no doubt it was rather too late in the season to be at these altitudes. As the afternoon was passing without any signs of the defaulting headmen or their animals, I sent Kallick to look for them, and find out whether they really meant to let us have animals or not. By nightfall he had not returned, and I became uneasy about him, but there was nothing to be done as the night was very dark, and it would have been useless to start to look for him with only a general idea of the direction in which he had gone.

27th November, Camp 98; 17 miles, 14,850 feet.—When we got up in the morning, there were still no signs of Kallick, and I was meditating on the advisability of starting to follow up his tracks in the snow, when some yaks and ponies were perceived on a hill-side being driven towards the camp. On getting a field-glass to bear, Kallick was discovered to be with them.

When he arrived in camp he said that the headman's tent was a long way off, and when he got there every one was in bed; however, by dint of shouting, they were aroused, and the headman coming to the door began speaking in a most haughty manner, asking, "Who are you and what do you want here? You shan't get any assistance from me, and the sooner you get out of the country the better for yourselves." To this was added a lot of abuse. Kallick's *forte* was bluff; at that game he was a match for any Tibetan. They appeared to have had a regular competition in profanity, the result being a total victory for Kallick, and the production of the animals.

Soon after starting, we struck a broad trail leading to Lhasa, on which we met numbers of Tibetans taking yaks laden with butter to market.

Our ponies were absolutely famishing, and began eating any filth found on the road. Several of them knocked up; it was heart-breaking having to abandon or shoot animals that had done us such good service, but whenever we happened to be near a tent I gave any animal that had no chance of getting on to the inhabitants in the hope that with care they might bring it round.

Our barley had nearly run out; only enough for

two small feeds remained, but it was spun out by the addition of tsampa, of which we had a fair supply, and more was procurable.

28th November, Camp 99 ; 24 miles, 14,950 feet.—A cloudy night, during which one pony died; during the day snow fell, thus making the chances of the ponies getting any grass worse than ever. Fortunately, at the place where we camped there was a sort of weed growing on a steep bank where the snow could not find a footing; there was not much of it, but enough to give them a scanty feed. The only chance of any of them living lay in the hope of our reaching a less inhospitable country within the next few days. The cook did not arrive in camp with us, so I sent two men back to look for him; they returned reporting no signs of him, so I sent off two more men, giving them some food and all our wine, consisting of about a couple of glasses of port which were kept in the medicine chest in case of emergency.

Next morning there were still no signs of the missing man, and the men who had gone to look for him had not returned; however, about 2 P.M. they all turned up. The cook's story was that he had been following behind the caravan when his pony lay down and died; he had tried to catch up the caravan on foot, but was too weak, so had sat down and passed the night on the hill-side. Fortunately he had a sheepskin robe, a blanket, and the thick padded saddle-cloth that was on the pony, otherwise he would assuredly have perished. As it was, his escaping without being frost-bitten was a marvel, as it was a windy night and some little time after day had broke the thermometer stood at 2°.

During the night I had taken observations for latitude — a terrible business fiddling about the screws of a very small theodolite with numbed fingers. The taking of observations all along was a great tax, and I did not get nearly as many as I should have liked to, as sometimes for days and even weeks together the sky was obscured, or the wind was so strong that a lamp would not burn. As we were always marching in the day-time, it was impossible to take solar observations.

30th November, Camp 100; 25 miles, 14,650 feet.—Very rough travelling all day over a country much cut up by ravines in which there were small streams running into a larger one, called the Lurung Chu, which had a general south-east direction. Three days' march down it there is said to be a country called Rong, in which trees are found; it is very possible, as on the march many bushes were seen, which looked as if we were going to come to trees soon.

On the road I shot a bear; the genus *Ursus* are not, as a rule, renowned for intelligence, but this was the biggest fool I have ever seen. When discovered, Dr. Thorold and myself with our ponies were full in his sight, about 200 yards off, with the wind blowing straight towards him. I fired a shot, the bullet going close over his back, but he only looked up, and then quietly continued his search for food, apparently quite unmoved; however, one through his back and another through his hip disposed of him. The fact is they are accustomed to see Tibetans, who are very frightened of them; and unlike the black buck of India, they have not learnt to discriminate between Europeans and natives. The guides told us they often attacked people—mauling them about the face in the same way that the Himalayan black bears do.

CHAPTER IX

ENTERING COUNTRY WITH STONE HOUSES

1st December, Camp 101; 9 miles, 13,210 feet; Tsuk Sun Dong Gong.—A long but easy ascent to the top of the Yag La pass, on which was an "obo"[1] gaily decorated with bright-coloured rags and flags, on which were printed prayers. On reaching it the Tibetans all shouted, and then fell to muttering prayers as hard as they could. The descent was mostly over snow, and was very steep; some of the yaks and ponies fell, but, marvellous to relate, in every case their fall fortunately was arrested before they got far. Looking at the descent either from above or below, it appeared that if any animal slipped, nothing would stop him until he had gone several thousand feet; and what would be the fate of a theodolite and other instruments on the back of an animal taking a flight through space of that distance and landing on jagged rocks? After getting over, we congratulated ourselves on having crossed from the side we did; had our fate led us to cross from

[1] Piles of stones ornamented with ragged flags found on the crests of all the principal passes in Tibet.

the other, the steep snowy side, the pass would have been a very troublesome obstacle. After leaving the snow, we entered a narrow valley, in which a herd of burhel were grazing, and some distance off, in some scrub jungle, I caught a glimpse of animals uncommonly like *goral* (Himalayan chamois, *Nemorrhedus goral*), but as it was a considerable distance and they were not long enough in sight to give me a chance of using a field-glass, they might possibly have been musk-deer—an animal one would more naturally expect to meet—but I remember distinctly at the time thinking that they were not musk-deer.

Turning to the south, down the valley of the Sok Chu, the monastery or gomba of Tsuk Sun Dong Gong suddenly came in sight, perched on an isolated rock. On approaching it, the village—a miserable collection of mud huts clustered at the foot of the rock—was seen. The whole thing exemplifies well the state of affairs in Tibet; the comfortable stately monastery in which the well-fed, well-dressed, priestly craft reside, and the miserable huts occupied by the poverty-stricken peasants, soul and body the slaves of the monks, crouching at the foot. The only chance of redemption for Tibet lies in foreign intercourse, and against such intercourse Lamas and Chinese will fight tooth and nail, well knowing that in the one case the iron rod with which they rule the people would shiver in their hands once foreigners appeared, and that in the other the enormous trade in twigs and waste foliage dignified with the name of tea would cease the day that free communication with the gardens of Assam and Darjiling was thrown open.

On first sighting the monastery no such thoughts crossed our minds, but simply pure joy at coming across the sight of a *house* once more after seeing nothing more substantial than nomads' tents for so long; the joy was heightened by some cultivation, and the only thing wanting to make the scene complete was trees. They were, doubtless, to be found somewhere close by, as amongst some fuel sent us were bits of what I took to be *Juniperus excelsa.*

After we had pitched our camp a man came over from the monastery to ask who we were and what we wanted; but as he was evidently a man of no rank, I sent him off, saying that if the headman of the place cared to come over, I should be delighted to have a talk with him, but I was not going to be cross-examined by every casual understrapper. This had the desired effect, and the big man speedily came over, apologising most profusely for his subordinate's conduct, and hoping that I was not angry. I told him I was not angry, but when business had to be done between two men, it was much better done without the intervention of a third party. He then asked the usual questions as to where we had come from and where we were going, suddenly breaking off to ask our ages. On being told, he was much astonished at our youth, as, in common with most orientals not accustomed to meet Europeans, he could not distinguish between a fair and a gray appearance.

After that, I asked him for transport animals. He agreed to give them, and promised to send men at once to collect them. This was very satisfactory, and with many bows he took his leave.

Afterwards Dr. Thorold went to the monastery, in the hope of being allowed to go over it, but was told that the only gate that it would be dignified for him to enter by was one which it was forbidden to open, as this would have the effect of causing the Yag La pass to become permanently closed. Lamas object to the inside of their monasteries being seen, principally, I think, on account of a not unnatural disinclination to allow the wealth they contain being known.

Round the monastery, and on the walls and chimneys of private houses, the horns of the Shoa-u-chu, or Tibetan stag, were to be seen. The natives said that they were to be found in Zama, Nakchu and on the road to Gyakundo, and that they live just above the tree line, not in the forests with which the lower parts of the hills are clothed.

2nd December, Camp 102; 15 miles, 13,425 feet.—In the morning a poor miserable-looking beggar, dressed in rags, came to our tents and saluted me with the Mahomedan salutation of *salaam aleikum* (peace be with you!). Much astonished, I gave the reply, *w'aleikum as salaam* (and with you be peace!), and calling to a caravan driver to interpret, asked who he was. He said he was a Chinese Mussulman, and had come into the country in the service of a mandarin; but they had been attacked by robbers. The others had managed to escape, but he had been taken prisoner. After plundering him of everything, even to the clothes on his back, the robbers had released him, and ever since he had been subsisting on the Tibetans' charity, but was very anxious to get out of the country. I told him that if he came with us, and was willing to work, he would receive food and clothes. He joyfully assented and was promptly enlisted.

TIBETAN LAMP.

Soon afterwards the headman turned up, bringing a present of four sheep, a brick of tea, a little gur, some butter, and a small piece of very inferior European cloth. In return I gave him some coral, a Kashmir cup, two silk handkerchiefs, some cloth, and ten rupees. He demurred a good deal to taking them, on the score that it was not right to take anything from a guest, and we were guests in the country. It was all play for the gallery; his scruples were easily overcome.

We made a very late start, as the promised yaks did not turn up till midday, and it was another hour before they were all loaded up. There are two bridges over the river at this place, one of the pattern common in the Himalayas, consisting of a succession of beams weighted down with stones sticking out from the bank, the lowest ones being the shortest and the top ones meeting. The other was made of iron chains formed of very long links without any cross bar. Both were out of repair, so we crossed on the ice.

The route lay up a valley called Ita, in which there is a river as large as the Tweed at Melrose, flowing into the Sok Chu. Owing to the late start, the sun was setting before we had covered 15 miles and reached the camping ground.

3rd December, Camp 103; 9 miles, 13,400 feet.—A very easy march to a place where there were a few huts situated close to the gomba or monastery of Pachung. These huts were built of stone, flat-roofed, and of a very substantial type. From this place two roads branched, one a northern one and the other a southern one. The evidence was most conflicting as to which of them was the better. The people that had come from Tsuk Sun Dong Gong maintained that the northern one was the better, and when put on oath, stuck to it; while the people here were as ready to freely swear that the northern route was almost impracticable, and the southern one was excellent. I decided to believe the people on the spot, for two reasons—one was that I thought it very probable that the Tsuk Sun Dong Gong people had been told by the monks to try and induce us to keep as far away from Lhasa territory as possible, the other, that both parties allowed that wild yak and kiang were found on the northern route—a fact which pointed to great elevation and intense cold.

4th December, Camp 104; 7 miles, 13,825 feet.—The yaks that we had been promised the previous evening did not turn up in the morning, but while we were breakfasting, the headman appeared, and approaching with many genuflections, presented the usual scarf of greeting, and in addition a brick of tea and a piece of cloth. He was a much more courtly old gentleman than most of his class, and after being seated, said he hoped we had not suffered many hardships on the road; to which I replied that although it had been very unpleasant on the Chang, now that we had arrived amongst a friendly people, our troubles were forgotten. We had more of the same style of profitable and edifying conversation, but at last I got him to business, and he said the promised yaks had been sent for and might arrive any minute. He also was kind enough to promise to send on an order that everything might be ready for us at the next stage. However they did not arrive until about one o'clock, when we continued our journey up the same valley, which is fairly thickly populated, the people living partly in houses and partly in tents.

5th December, Camp 105; 25 miles, 14,060 feet.—Though a long march, it was by no means a tiresome one, as we did it very comfortably. The yaks were all loaded in the dark, and with the first streak of light were started; then we had our breakfast, and the cooking things were sent off. On our ponies we caught up the caravan, and passing it, came to a sheltered sunny ravine in which we had tea, and then

MONASTERY OF TSUK SUN DONG GONG.

throwing ourselves down, smoked the pipe of peace, while the caravan came up and passed on. After allowing it to get well ahead, we mounted and followed, catching it up just as the camping ground was reached.

Two tents had been pitched for us, a lot of fuel collected, and the inhabitants bowing and sticking out their tongues welcomed us, while the chief amongst them came forward with a scarf of greeting. The pansang of Ita had evidently been as good as his word in regard to sending on a letter directing that we should be treated with honour.

This was a most agreeable change after travelling through a country in which every stranger was regarded not only as a possible, but a very probable enemy. These people were anxious to know in what way they might be of use, and bustled round, helping to unload animals, pitching tents, and lighting fires. The climate had also become much milder, which added considerably to the amenities of travelling. During the night the thermometer did not go below zero, and there was little wind; it seemed as if, so far as we ourselves were concerned, the worst was over; but the poor ponies were still suffering; two having died on the march. The appearance of the country had entirely changed, steep valleys and snowy peaks taking the place of the low rounded hills that become monotonous to the traveller on the high plateaux.

We got into camp about 4 P.M., and as the

natives said there were bears about, Dr. Thorold went out to look for one; he saw no bears but was lucky enough to find a herd of six Shoa-u-chu stags, and killed one and wounded another; so we decided to halt for a day in order to follow up the wounded one, hoping some more would also be found. Dr. Thorold had a long day's tracking in the snow before coming on the wounded one he was after, but he got it all right. I trudged about the whole day over hills covered with bushes and a foot of snow, without even seeing the tracks of one; so I fancy they are pretty rare.

7th December, Camp 106; 9 miles, 13,325 feet. —Trees at last. As we descended the valley, we found the sides well clothed with *Juniperus excelsa*, many of them of large size; the whole caravan were delighted; since leaving the Indus valley in June we had not seen a single tree, and it seemed now as if our troubles were over. With water in the valleys and fuel that the snow could not hide on the hill-sides, there was nothing to fear.

A new lot of birds were also to be seen; the ravens had disappeared, and in their place the equally ruffianly magpies were hopping about, while water ouzels and robins were plentiful.

The camp tents were pitched for us; they were of the ordinary Tibetan pattern, made of rough black sacking, an extremely porous material, and as they were uncommonly ragged, having holes big enough for a man to crawl through, except for the honour and glory of the thing, one might as well have been in the open. The one in which I slept had a furze bush thrust into the biggest hole—a poor protection against a Tibetan wind.

As we arrived early, Dr. Thorold and myself, taking a couple of Tibetans with us, went out to look for stags, but failed to find any.

8th December, Camp 107, Richando; 25 miles, 13,225 feet.—Before we left, the pansang turned up and asked for a letter, stating that he had given our party all the assistance required. I did so, and he insisted on my annexing my seal to it. He then began a long story about how the neighbouring pansangs were a grade higher in rank than he was, and what an injustice it was, and would I use my influence to have it remedied? It was no use explaining that I was not the donor of rank in those parts; he insisted upon it that, when I reached China, I had only to say the word and everything would be rectified. Another of his grievances was that the Deva Zhung's people were continually encroaching and seizing territory that by rights belonged to Chinese subjects in his district; two valleys had thus been annexed. It was no use appealing to the Amban at Lhasa, as he was completely in the hands of the Tibetans, and neither could nor would do anything. The mysterious power that Asiatics in out-of-the-way places attribute to Europeans is a curious study, and accounts for the success that has often attended adventurers.

From this place a road runs south through a place called Gya Rang, in which there are said to be Chinese shops, and rejoins the Chiamdo road, two marches farther on; it was said to be much easier than the one we elected to take as being the shortest.

9th December, Camp 108, Pata Samdo; 21 miles, 13,325 feet.—The Richando people said that on this march there were two passes, both very difficult; there certainly were two passes, but no one accustomed to the passes of the Western Himalayas would for a moment consider them difficult. At Pata Samdo, which is situated on the banks of the Mo Chu, there were a few houses, outside of which there were scaffoldings decorated with hay made into ropes to be used as fodder for the animals when the ground was under snow. The people contrasted very unfavourably with those we had left behind in the Ita valley; in insolence and inquisitiveness they were nearly as bad as their Chinese brethren. The elder men apparently hid themselves, and the younger ones displayed a mixture of affected good-fellowship and buffoonery that was nothing but sheer insolence. Dignity, which is so marked a feature in most orientals, was utterly wanting. To add to the amenities of travel, as the country became more civilised, beggars appeared pestering us at every camp.

For some mysterious reason they seemed determined to hide from us all information about the sport to be got in the country; one man was telling a caravan driver that there were many bears about, when another man coming up said, "Don't tell him anything about them." The original speaker then in the most barefaced manner denied all he had said, and promptly swore there was not a bear in the country, and all subsequent inquiries were met by the invariable negative *Mārē.* However, we determined to halt for a day, in order to give the ponies a rest, and spend it looking for game.

The first thing to do—after announcing our intention of halting in any case, so that there could be no possible incentive to lie, in the hopes of making us move on—was to make inquiries, holding out hopes of substantial rewards being forthcoming in the event of game being shown. We certainly thought the idea of reward had done the needful, as some men came forward and promised to show us stags, and it was clearly explained to them that we did not want and would not fire at musk-deer; they said they understood, and would show us stags. Dr. Thorold then started down the valley with a couple of men, and I started up, passing some scattered hamlets, out of which some big dogs rushed barking and snapping; that the art of throwing stones had been neglected in my education was a source of much regret. Having learned by experience that stones did not pay, I armed myself with a powerful cudgel; and it was fortunate I did so, as on approaching the next hamlet a pack rushed out, headed by a brute the perfect image of a wolf.

He differed from the others in having a fixed determination to make his charge good, and came right in on me; but a cut across the snout as he made a spring reduced his ardour, and as we pursued our way his howls reverberated through the valley.

When we reached the head of the main valley, the guides turned up a small side one, in which there were some huts and obviously no stags. I told them that this nullah could not possibly hold stags; they said, "Certainly it does not, but there are plenty of musk-deer." What was to be done with people of that sort? Before leaving camp it had been carefully explained to them that I did not want, and would not fire at, musk-deer, and they had faithfully promised to take me to stag ground, and now they denied the whole thing. I returned to camp and went in for another cross-examination. Most of the people said that stags only came in summer, and at this time of year there were none anywhere near, but one man said he knew a valley not far off in which there might be some. Determined not to leave a stone unturned, I started off, taking two men with me. On reaching it we followed it up as far as the unbroken snow, without seeing anything except a musk-deer, which I refused to fire at. Just where the vegetation ended we sat down, lit a fire and had some tea, after which we retraced our steps to camp, getting in just at dark, not having even seen a stag's tracks; they must be somewhere, but when the natives either cannot or

TIBETAN DANCERS.

M

will not give any assistance, it takes time to find out where that somewhere is, and time is just the thing above all others we could not afford to waste; the middle of December was late to be amongst these mountains.

11th December, Camp 109; 21 miles, 14,100 feet.—The road led through a perfect maze of mountains and over two passes, neither of which, however, was very difficult. On the road we met an enormous number of pilgrims going to Lhasa; all of them, men, women, and children, were on foot, with their belongings on their backs, and very heavy loads they appeared to be. Many of them carried flags, on which prayers were written, and in every man's hand was a spear.

We pitied the poor little mites of children, and wondered how they ever could accomplish the long and difficult journey before them; but faith is a great factor, and in their case we hoped it would remove mountains. I expect, if the truth was known, the mortality on the road amongst them is something enormous.

12th December, Camp 110; 13 miles, 12,063 feet—Sari Samdu.—Two other passes, but like the former ones fairly easy, and then into the valley of the Sa Chu, a fairly large stream, which in summer must be quite unfordable. There were the remains of a bridge, but quite out of repair. Two days' march up the river there are said to be people who own allegiance neither to China nor Lhasa, and beyond them is the Chang. The village of Sari Samdu is situated at the junction of three valleys; the hill-sides are covered with patches of cultivation and small hamlets, many of which are situated very high up. The limit of cultivation seems generally to be about 13,500 feet.

There were some Zhos, hybrids between cows and yaks, about, and also a large number of ordinary cattle, a great change in the fauna. We managed to get some chopped straw for the ponies, which was a great thing, as insufficient nutriment was what was killing them. Once more it was demonstrated to me that civility is thrown away on Tibetans. I asked them to sell some first of all, promising a good price, and only received impertinence in exchange. I then demanded in an imperious tone that it be supplied at once; the result was that their whole tone changed, and it was promptly produced. The only way to get things in Tibet is by bullying, and in the morning, the last thing before starting, hand over a liberal amount as payment; directly they receive payment they at once begin to think you are weak and become impertinent, so it must be postponed till the last moment. But it must not be supposed that we never received civility in Tibet,—as I have shown, in some places the people were very nice and exceedingly attentive, but going east they seem to be strongly infected with some of the worst traits in the Chinese character, and isolated villagers here and there were particularly bad.

A great misfortune happened to us in a tent being blown down, thus breaking a thermometer and leaving only one, which I determined to keep securely locked up to be only used for astronomical and boiling-point observations.

13th December, Camp 111; 10 miles.—Down the easternmost of the three valleys meeting at Sari Samdu a fairly broad stream flowed, carrying lumps of ice; it was curious to see such a large stream flowing in a westerly direction, but somewhere below Sari Samdu it must take a turn in a south-easterly direction.

The road was the first we had seen to which anything had been done by the hand of man. The few roads and paths hitherto come across only owed their existence to the effect produced on the soil by the feet of men and animals, but here was one with evident signs of a considerable amount of labour having been expended on it. At the curves the hills had been dug out, and where there were fields on either hand it ran between stone walls: here and there it bifurcates where a *mānė́* or heap of stones with sacred inscriptions is met, so as to allow people coming from either direction to pass, leaving it on whichever side is accordant with their belief. The Sari Samdu people belong to the Pembu sect, and always leave one on their left, thus differing from the Ladakhis, who leave one on their right. They also turn their prayer-wheels in the reverse direction. Tibet is a good deal split up amongst these rival sects of Pembu and Pindah; often one is in the morning amongst people of one kind and in the evening amongst the other. There is a good deal of rivalry and bad feeling between them.

So far as trees went we were improving, and opposite our camp was a patch of what are called Tongsing in Ladakhi and Ri in Hindustani; a sort of fir.

A troupe of professional dancers gave us a performance. The first part was much the same as the masked dance at Hemis but without the masks. They began by walking round in slow time, striking a drum and chanting a mournful dirge, then the time quickened, and round and round they whirled in true dancing dervish style till they had to stop for want of breath. They then danced a variety of the same figure, in which one of them had two swords in each hand and turned somersaults; and in the third act, one of them had a five-stringed banjo, on which he played a tune with remarkably few notes in it. After they had been rewarded and had departed, another troupe, consisting of two men and a boy, sat down in front of the tents, and removing the cover with much solemnity, disclosed to view an umbrella-like arrangement decorated with bright beads and lumps of bone. This was slowly turned round, while a terribly mournful sound—tune I cannot call it—was given forth by the company; they were hastily rewarded and requested to move on. The reward was purposely fixed on a low scale to discourage others, but still it must have been too high, as no sooner had they gone than an ugly old woman took their place, and disclosing similar paraphernalia, began, in the most unmusical voice I have ever heard, to chant a dirge appalling in its mournfulness; she also was hastily induced to move on, and as her song ceased, we felt a relief like the sudden cessation of pain.

CHAPTER X

DESERTED BY THE GUIDES

After we had left Sari Samdu the four Tibetans of much-vaunted faithfulness, supplied by the Lhasa people to accompany us to Ta Chen Lu, managed to make their escape, taking with them eleven ponies and a few other unconsidered trifles. Their defection was not discovered for some time; so they managed to get a good start. When it was discovered I sent four caravan drivers to follow them up, but they had the best of their pursuers, as, having so many ponies, they were able to ride on four and drive the others, and whenever a ridden one knocked up they mounted another and abandoned the one that was done up. Our men were out all that day and the following night, without succeeding in overtaking them. Before giving up the search they induced some Tibetans by offers of a big reward to continue it, and then returned to camp much exhausted. They had recovered eight ponies, found abandoned, and left them at a Tibetan's house to be fed and brought on as soon as they had sufficiently rested to be able to march.

The Tibetans who continued the search came upon the deserters, forced them to abandon all their property — not only the three ponies belonging to us, but four that were their own—and take to the mountains with nothing but the clothes they had on and their matchlocks and swords. Misguided men, they had been promised not only good pay on reaching Ta Chen Lu, but compensation for any pony they might lose on the way. Now they had been stripped of everything and were left to wander in the mountains without food, money, tents, or horses. Although they had committed a distinct crime in stealing the animals, and shown deliberate unfaithfulness, still I could not help feeling sorry for the plight they were left in, and hoped that by selling their swords and matchlocks they would realise sufficient to enable them to reach their homes.

Two of them, I believe, had at one time done a little in the Chukpa line of business, more in an amateur than professional way, and one of them had been caught and got off after having to disgorge half his plunder, a rather insufficient punishment and scarcely likely to act powerfully as a deterrent.

15th December, Camp 112; 8 miles, 12,825 feet—Tashi Ling.—During the night one mule and two ponies were stolen. The people tried to make out that they had strayed, but their ropes had most unmistakably been cut with a knife. The ponies were no great loss, but losing the mule was a serious matter; it was one of the best animals in the caravan.

The promised transport was a long time turning up, so it was very late before we started, but the march, which was up a valley fairly well populated, was a short one, so it did not much matter.

The camp was at the village of Tashi Ling, close to a monastery perched on a rock.

The people were exceedingly troublesome, mobbing us in regular Chinese fashion, and displaying a stubborn sort of insolence. One of them, whom Dr. Thorold asked to step back, drew a sword and looked like using it. Thorold, who was unarmed, promptly struck him with his fists; for a few seconds it looked as if there was going to be a free fight. Stones and clods of hard earth were thrown into the camp, while snow-scrapers, which were lying about, were promptly seized by those who had no better arms. Then there was a pause, and both parties stood looking at each other; we hesitated to use breech-loaders, knowing the dreadful effect they would have on a crowd of people, and they evidently did not like the idea of attempting to rush the camp, so it ended peaceably, which was fortunate for all concerned. The headman of the village was present at the time, but he appeared to have no influence whatever, though his intentions were of the best.

The headman of the district, who was in the village, had sent a scarf of welcome and an iron vessel full of chang,[1] with an apology for not coming himself, as he was too drunk, but would come in the morning. It appears there was also another headman, who sent an emissary to procure a certificate stating that we had been well treated in the district, to which I replied that his district I believed extended for two days' march more, and on reaching the boundary he would get a certificate according to the way we were treated. The gomba or monastery is said to be under the Deva Zhung, but the people are under China; it is only a nominal rule, and practically they may be said to be independent.

16th December, Camp 113; 27 miles, 12,672 feet.—After striking our tents we sat for a long time on our baggage waiting for the promised transport, while a crowd of people stared at us. They brought a great many musk pods for sale, many of which were obviously adulterated. At last the transport animals arrived, and we started, very glad to get out of a place in which it was so difficult to avoid getting into a row. The road, which was over a pass and down a valley, was very bad going, and as we were benighted long before reaching our destination, it was a very trying march.

On approaching the village of Tinchin, which is situated on a hill and presents a very fort-like appearance, we were met by men carrying flaming

[1] A sort of beer much drunk in Tibet.

pine branches, who led us through the village to an open patch of ground where we were to camp. The mob were annoying, crowding round us, and even when we got our tents up and went into them we were not left alone. However they were good-natured, and if it had not been that they were continually trying to slip away with things and actually did manage to steal a couple of bags containing clothes, we should not have much minded them.

Amongst the crowd there were two Chinamen, the first we had seen, and in the village there were some pigs,—where the Chinaman is found there is the pig also.

A very striking feature in the village was the number of children. In Western Tibet the absence of children, which is owing to the prevalence of polyandry, is very noticeable, but in these parts polyandry is not practised, and as a consequence the villages are as full of children as are those in India.

17th December, Camp 114; 4 miles, 12,762 feet. —A ridiculously small march, not enough for a decent afternoon stroll; it was very annoying, as we wanted to get through the belt of country occupied by these exceedingly disagreeable people as quickly as possible. The only way to march with any degree of comfort would be to leave one camp before daylight and reach the next after dark; getting in early, one is exposed to annoyances from a particularly disagreeable mob as long as daylight lasts. It was no use speaking to them good-naturedly, as the only response was shouts of laughter and abuse, and, brave in their numbers and innocent of the power of our firearms, on being spoken roughly to they would promptly fly to arms.

Their headmen appeared to be quite powerless with them.

18th December, Camp 115; 13 miles, 12,825 feet.—Before leaving, I managed to exchange four worn-out ponies for two well-conditioned ones: it was a good bargain for both parties—for me as the ponies could not possibly have gone much farther, and for the Tibetans as they got four ponies that with a couple of months' rest and good food would be at least as good as those they gave.

As at Tashi Ling, great quantities of musk were brought for sale; they began by asking twenty rupees a pod, but eventually came down to three pods for seven rupees.

After loading up we started amidst a general clamour for baksheesh from people who had done nothing but annoy us. Our course for a mile or two lay down the side of a river, and then crossing it by a wooden bridge and bearing away to the east, Baru, at which there is a most picturesque monastery on the top of a very steep isolated hill, was reached. There we changed animals and went on for another five miles. As we approached the village at which we were to halt, a number of men appeared, who had come to induce us to go somewhere else. To strengthen their arguments they had brought guns with them, but everything was settled peaceably, and we were allowed to proceed.

The whole march was through magnificent scenery, a wide valley in which monasteries and villages were scattered about, some of them high up on the mountains, perched in places apparently inaccessible to anything without wings. Cultivation extended to a considerable height on both sides, and behind a glorious panorama of snowy peaks formed a background. Man alone was vile; wherever we went we were mobbed, and as every man was a thief, it was impossible to prevent things being stolen while loading or unloading the animals. The utmost we could do was to keep a good look-out on the boxes containing money, books, and instruments.

19th December, Camp 116; 12 miles, 12,425 feet.—The custom about these parts is, for each village of a certain size to supply transport to the next one, a plan that is liable to involve very small marches; but on this occasion, when we arrived at the changing place, animals were ready for us, and the people having heard that we were a strong well-armed party, were only too willing to pass us on as quickly as possible, fearing we should lay them under contributions according to Eastern fashion. Had they known that there were only five guns in the party, possibly they would not have been so prompt in supplying transport. It is needless to say we had no wish to inflict our company on them more than we could help.

At night, about 11 o'clock, a caravan driver woke me up with the news that a Tibetan villager had reported seven armed men in a ravine close by, who were evidently watching the camp with the intention of attacking it when every one was asleep. I sent out some men to search the nullahs, and they returned reporting having seen thirty men, all armed, lying *perdus*, close by.

The first thing to do was to see that arms and ammunition were all handy. Our battery consisted of two double ·500 Express rifles, two Martini-Henry cavalry carbines, and one fowling-piece, quite enough to manage thirty Tibetans with, if we were not taken by surprise; but that was the fear, and strategically, the position of our camp was bad, being quite in the open, and from whatever side the assailants approached, they would have cover. Close by there was a walled enclosure, a faulty position also, as it was commanded by the roofs of some neighbouring houses — a decidedly bad business if the villagers were in league with the assailants, but as they had given the information, it looked as if they were not disposed to turn against us. But even if we had had less reason to believe the villagers reliable, the enclosure was the only place we could get cover for both horses and men, and, bad as it was, it was the best the country offered, so we moved everything into it, and after posting a couple of sentries, went to sleep.

20th December, Camp 117, Maru; 15 miles, 12,250 feet.—The Chukpas, or whoever the gentlemen were who had been stalking us, evidently did not dare to attack our position with no chance of taking us by surprise, so we were left undisturbed.

A few half-starved cattle turned up in the morning to carry our things, and a crowd of men, women, and children to act as porters. They fought and wrangled amongst themselves for an hour or two over the allotment of the packages. The matter was eventually settled, as such discussions usually are, by the strong men walking off with the light articles, leaving the weaklings and women and children to bring on the heavy ones. It was a terribly long day, and we did not get in till dark, as they stopped at every house for chang and conversation, and it was always difficult to get them going again. Towards the end of the march we crossed a bridge and entered a country under the Deva Zhung's jurisdiction. The change in the attitude of the people was at once apparent; the identical people under the rule of China differ enormously from those under Lhasa. The Lhasa Government may not be a strong one but, compared to the Chinese, it seems so; thieves, instead of being the rule, are the exception, and the people can certainly be restrained and kept in order by those in authority over them. A good deal of it may be owing to the fact that the Tibetan of high rank is immeasurably superior to the Chinese mandarin — in intellect his equal, in strength of character his superior; there is a more manly healthy tone about him than about the time-serving literati of the Celestial Empire.

21st December, Camp 118; 19 miles, 14,325 feet.—We started by a gradual ascent through fields for the first part to the Nam La Pass, and then a slight descent took us into a valley in which there were a few patches of cultivation. Then gradually ascending, just before dark we camped on a bitterly cold spot well above the bush level.

22nd December, Camp 119; 12 miles, 13,800 feet.—Crossed a pass, on the north side of which there was a great deal of snow, but on the whole it was easy, and camped close to the tents of some nomads who are Chinese subjects. An official who had come with us from Maru, announcing his intention of seeing us safely to the boundary of his district, which was seven marches distant, now announced that this was the boundary, and he was not going any farther. One of the things in which the Deva Zhung's Tibetans do not excel the Chinese Tibetans is truthfulness, for both lie equally freely. But that is not the fault of the Government; our own in India has always been the admiration of the world, but I never heard that our Law Courts have done anything to promote truthfulness amongst the people.

23rd December, Camp 120; 15 miles, 13,025 feet.—As we heard stags were to be got on the road, Dr. Thorold and myself started off in front of the caravan in the hopes of seeing some. As we descended the valley, the country became very gamey-looking; the lower parts of the hills were covered with *Juniperus excelsa* and above were bushes in snow; that is the sort of place to find stags. We were, however, unfortunate in not seeing any, though

THE SHAGGA (*CROSSOPTILON TIBETANUM*).

musk-deer were exceedingly plentiful, and also white pheasants, called "shagga" in Tibet (*Crossoptilon tibetanum*); they are large handsome birds, but terribly hard to kill; the only chance of getting them is a pellet through the head. I carefully stalked a flock of them, and getting close, knocked feathers out of some most freely, but they went away apparently none the worse; following them up again I managed to bag one, but several more went away hit; it was very annoying wasting cartridges, and especially as in no case had I taken any but the easiest of pot shots. They were all feeding amongst juniper bushes, and the crop of the one I got was full of the berries. Their cry is a whirring sound, varied occasionally by a short cluck, and they are generally found in flocks of about thirty. Lower down we often found them in the fields close to houses. As I descended from the hills with the bird in my hand, I was met by a number of men with guns who had come out to stop the shooting; they said that if any animals were shot, everybody living in the valley would become ill. They are a terribly superstitious people, and in their superstition are apt to become dangerous.

One of our Ladakhis had a long conversation with one of the guides on the road on the subject of marriage in these parts. The bridegroom usually gives only about five sheep for his wife; ruling rates in the west are much higher.

24th December, Camp 121; 17 miles, 12,265 feet. About 2 miles beyond Riuchi.—Started by crossing a pass which was a stiffish pull, and then descended into a beautiful well-wooded valley in which numbers of pheasants were running about. From the pass the town of Riuchi, apparently all monastery, is seen; a huge pagoda-like erection is the most conspicuous object; while round it are the monks' quarters, solid-looking buildings painted in bright stripes of red, white, and black. On approaching the village or town a collection of miserable mud-huts is discovered. As we neared it a man, professing to be one in authority, met us, and said that farther on arrangements had been made for our reception. Believing him we went on, but after going a couple of miles past the town, we began to understand that it was only a plan to prevent us halting near the monastery, so I gave the order to camp. The man who had met us, however, had got some distance ahead, and the caravanbashi was with him; they reached a village when the guide suddenly disappeared, while the people turned out and threatening the caravanbashi, said they would not allow him to advance a yard farther in their territory. As he could not alter their determination, he returned to where we had camped. Later on another headman coming to our camp, I upbraided him with the treatment we were receiving, telling him that we were only peaceful travellers with no wish to hurt any one; but at the same time, I was careful not to take too mild a tone, knowing the bad effect that always had. He departed promising that all our wishes should be attended to.

However, next day the promised yaks had not turned up in the morning, so we were obliged to halt—a thing we were not sorry to do, as it was Christmas-day. Altogether it was a red-letter day, for here we were in a warm sunny valley at a low altitude, with a larder remarkably well stocked with three partridges, two pheasants, and a saddle of venison; an epicure could not wish for more. Besides about two oz. of sugar were discovered, so, with the addition of some of the worst raisins I have ever seen, that had been given to us by a headman some stages back, a plum-pudding was concocted, and a real good plum-pudding it was. The cellar was not so well furnished as the larder, but Dr. Thorold had a small flask of coca-wine, which we drank to "absent friends."

26th December, Camp 122; 25 miles, 12,500 feet.—Through the most lovely country over which it has ever been my lot to travel. The path ran through a forest a hundred or two feet above the river, with here and there open grassy patches with trees scattered about. Each bend in the river disclosed to view a panorama of surpassing beauty. In no part of Kashmir does the beauty of the scenery excel that of this part of Tibet.

Game is plentiful, but shooting is forbidden in all the country having any connection with the monastery of Riuchi.

On the road we passed a place where iron-smelting was being carried on. The abundance of fuel furnished by the forests makes it feasible here, but undoubtedly there are many places in Tibet where there is plenty of ore, though owing to the absence of fuel nothing can be made of it.

27th December, Camp 123; 16 miles, 12,325 feet —Memda.—At this place there was a Tibetan official, who was the real headman of the place, and a Chinese detachment of half a dozen or so soldiers under the command of one of their countrymen, whose position and rank were equal, I suppose, to about that of a sergeant. He came to call on us, bringing a present of a sheep, some vegetables, and two jugs of wine; the latter was of the usual Chinese kind. He was an intelligent man, and had heard of and knew a good deal about Calcutta and Darjiling. As his rank was not high—and it is always necessary to stand on one's dignity with Chinese—instead of returning his call, I sent a couple of men, after his departure, to him with a present of a gold coin in return for what he had given us. He was delighted at receiving it, as well he might be, considering it was worth about five times the value of his gifts.

CROSSOPTILON LEUCURUM (see page 296).

CHAPTER XI

IN THE NEIGHBOURHOOD OF CHIAMDO

28th December, Camp 124; 15 miles, 12,400 feet.—Just before starting an emissary from Chiamdo arrived, and in rather a peremptory manner informed us that we were to go by a southern route. I told him we were going by the straight route, and no other. He did not attempt to argue any farther, though he decidedly had the whip-hand of us, as he might very easily have forced us to go any road he liked by refusing to supply transport for any other; as it was we got the transport all right, and started on the straight road to Chiamdo. The country was still just as beautiful as it had been the few previous days. Bright sky, bracing air, and lovely scenery, and the only thing wanted to make it an absolutely perfect country to travel in, is a less suspicious people.

Half-way we stopped and changed animals, taking advantage of the halt to have tea. On arrival at the staging place we were accommodated in a Chinaman's house; it had a square courtyard in the middle, in which the horses stood, and having latticed windows pasted over with paper, was very snug; as it was the first time we had slept under a roof for over six months, we were quite disposed to appreciate it. There were some rather dirty mattresses about, and being of a suspicious nature, we thought it advisable to have them removed and sleep on the boards.

Our host presented us with some mutton and wine; the mutton, though apparently a long time killed, was not at all high, but very much dried up.

We were told that the Amban at Chiamdo was sending a man to meet us, which was a polite way of saying he was sending a man to stop us. The one or two Chinamen in the place were exceedingly civil, saying, in the most friendly way, that the Chinese and English were brothers, but that the Tibetans, who were only savages, were quite outside the brotherhood, and would endeavour in every way to deceive us, though, of course, all the Chinese in the country would do what they could to help us. The Chinese occasionally in out-of-the-way places are very civil.

29th December, Camp 125; 31 miles, 11,125 feet.—Began the march by crossing the Namcho La pass, which was a stiff pull, even for the yaks, and one pony died on the top.

Descending we came to a sort of a custom-house, where there were several Chinese, one of whom asked us in and gave us a dish of minced meat. The house had a very peaceful homely appearance, with shelves on the walls, on which cups were arranged, while hanging up were some brass spoons, well polished; it also boasted a table and several forms. The Tibetan wife of the master of the house, a good-looking young woman, was continually bustling backwards and forwards, looking after the children, of whom she seemed to have a quiverful. The most striking thing about her was that she had departed from the customs of her country sufficiently to have washed her face. She gave us four eggs, which were a great treat, as they were the first we had seen for many a long day.

Near the village of Lamdo there were two apologies for tents ready for us, and some chopped straw for our horses. As soon as we got into the camp the villagers, with the headman as their spokesman, appeared, and presenting some butter, prostrated themselves on the ground, and petitioned that I would not lay heavy requisitions on them, as they were a very poor people, and the land barely furnished sufficient for their sustenance. I was graciously pleased to accede to their request, and they departed much relieved and with many expressions of thankfulness. The relief to me occasioned by their departure was no less, as the whole thing was so absurd that it was only with difficulty I kept my countenance and refrained from bursting out laughing. The idea of our small party, whose only wish was to get through the country as peacefully and quietly as possible, laying it under contributions, was too ridiculous. After they had gone a man arrived from Chiamdo, requesting that we would take a route passing to the north of the town, but I refused to do so. He then asked us to halt for a couple of days, in order that he might communicate with his superiors, but I would not agree to that either. He had a long story about how there were both Pindahs and Pembus in the place, and how each would blame the other for bringing us in if we advanced any farther, and disturbances would be sure to ensue.

30th December, Camp 126, outside Chiamdo.—Before we had started in the morning, the same official came to our tents, trying hard to induce us to stop, if only for a few hours, as some Lamas of high rank were expected to arrive from Chiamdo during the day; but I declined to do so, as our only chance of getting to Chiamdo at all lay in pushing on, so we loaded up and marched, accompanied by several Tibetans, whose horses were covered with bells, which kept up a continual jingling. On the road we stopped at a small village, and had tea in a Chinaman's house, and the two Chinese soldiers accompanying us were changed for two others. The ones relieved promptly got their opium pipes out, and throwing themselves down on a settle, proceeded to enjoy the fragrant narcotic.

After we had finished our tea, we remounted and continued our journey. On approaching Chiamdo we were met by a church dignitary, evidently of very high rank, arrayed in red garments ornamented with gold embroidery and with a yellow cap on his head. On getting near he dismounted, and presenting a scarf of welcome, said that the Amban had sent him with a request that we would be good enough to halt for a little at a house close by. I agreed to this, and he galloped back whence he had come. We proceeded more leisurely, and on arrival at some barn-like buildings close to a bridge dismounted, and were ushered in, numbers of Lamas crowding round us.

We were kept waiting there a few minutes, and were getting very impatient at the delay, when the Amban appeared. He was an extremely girlish-looking youth, appearance, manners, voice, and everything about him truly feminine: his mincing gait as he advanced holding out his hand in a most extraordinary but no doubt very fashionable manner, quite took me aback. As soon as we were all seated, he asked whence we had come and where we were going. After being told he suddenly rose up and went out, leaving us with the Lamas, a much more stiff-necked and difficult lot to deal with. They were a strikingly able and intellectual-looking set of men; the two head ones especially had faces that would arrest attention anywhere. Education and the habit of ruling had no doubt done a good deal to mark men gifted by nature with talents above the ordinary run of their fellow-countrymen. They plunged at once into business, and said that, come what might, they would not allow us to proceed along the road to China passing through Chiamdo, but they would give us every assistance if we would go by the route passing to the north, which had been followed by M. Bonvalôt and his companions. I told them I was determined to go straight on, and would not turn to the north for any one; as for Chiamdo, that it happened to be in the way was unfortunate, as I was not anxious to see it, and if they liked I would promise not to enter any monastery. But we were going to China; this was the straight road, and I would go by it, and no other. They would not agree to this at all, and began threatening, saying, "Advance, if you dare; we have three thousand men with guns, and will soon stop you." I said, "All right; if you want fighting, you will get it; but straight forward we are going." Voices were being raised, both parties getting very angry; and it looked as if the fighting was going to begin then and there, when the Amban entered and peace was restored; he got the Lamas to leave the room, promising to settle the question with us. He was very easy to deal with, and inclined to agree to anything; but was terribly afraid of the Lamas. It was very evident that his authority was only a mere shadow. The arrangement come to with him was that we were not to enter the town, but to skirt it, rejoining the road on the farther side.

Soon after he had taken his departure, he sent a man over saying he would like to have a talk with us quietly when no one was about, and would we receive him some time after dark. I sent back a message saying we should be delighted to see him at any time that he cared to come. About 9 P.M. he came over, and after we had seated him and given him tea, the conversation began. He assumed an extremely confidential tone, and said he should like to do everything in his power for us; that the English and Chinese were like brothers, and great friendship existed between their respective Governments; but the Lamas were a very turbulent set, and he really had no power at all, otherwise he would have taken us into Chiamdo and shown all the hospitality that was in his power. He trusted that we would realise the position in which he was placed, and pardon his apparent want of friendliness. I told him that it was evident what sort of people he had to deal with, and we quite understood his position.

31st December, Camp 127.—Soon after daylight we received a message from the Amban to say he was ready and waiting for us, so that we might start together. We hurried over a very scanty breakfast and rushed down to the courtyard below, only to find no sign of the Amban, and a man came out from his quarters to ask us to wait a little. No doubt the great man would dearly have loved to have had us dancing attendance on his doorstep for half an hour or so for the edification of the onlookers. But it was not the first time I had had dealings with the Chinese, or had tricks of the same nature tried on, so I sent a message to say we were going on and he could follow when he liked.

The big road crossing the bridge runs straight

through the town, so we took a smaller one which runs down the right bank of the river, winding in and out along the shoulders of the mountains. After we had gone a few miles, the Amban with a brilliant staff of Lamas and a few Chinamen caught us up; he had had a spill from his horse on the way, but was not much the worse of it.

We passed close to the town, with nothing but the river between us and it. The people were gathered on the flat roofs of the houses to stare at us. As we passed looking at the crowd, it appeared as if they were all Lamas and Chinamen.

The town is situated on two ledges at the junction of two rivers, of which the easternmost is the larger. On the higher of the two ledges there are two very fine monasteries with roofs liberally adorned with gilding; the houses, which are whitewashed, are all flat-roofed, and there is a general Maltese-like look about the place. I should be inclined at a rough guess to estimate the population at 12,000, and according to what we were told, 3000 of them are monks. Just below the town there is a bridge over the river, but we went farther down, and crossing on the ice turned up a side valley. After going for a few miles we came to the village where we were to halt. On dismounting we were shown into a room, and tea, milk, and some excellent unleavened bread were produced, which after our long ride we thoroughly appreciated. Before our things had come up, the Amban, who had quarters in a neighbouring house, came to visit us, bringing a minor official with him; the conversation was of the usual sort, consisting of continual reiterations of the statement that the English and Chinese were brothers, and would always help each other, etc. Before leaving he said that he had something very particular to say, and would like to pay us a visit later on. As he had been complaining that the fall from his horse had given him a slight shaking, I told him not to trouble himself, as we would go over to his quarters in the evening; he said he would esteem it a great honour if we did so.

A curious thing amongst the Chinese in these parts is the number of old British regimental buttons they wear, many of them belonging to Hindustani and Punjab regiments whose names have long since vanished from the Army List. On one man's coat I saw three buttons, respectively stamped 16th P.I., 5th P.I., and 12th P.I. (Punjab Infantry).

In the evening we went over to see the Amban, as we had promised. On entering we were seated on high straight-backed chairs, and provided with tea. He asked what was our intention, to halt or go on in the morning. I said that we would halt for a couple of days for the ponies' sake, to which he agreed, saying he would see that arrangements were made for our being properly supplied with everything needful during the two days. Shortly afterwards some Lamas entered, and begged him to induce us to leave at once. He asked us to do so, and the Lamas retired to leave him to settle the matter with us. I said we would meet them half-way, and only halt for one day instead of two, as had been our original intention. He thought it quite fair, and said he would inform the Lamas that it had been settled in that way. We departed after that, and reaching our quarters, went to bed. Just as I was dozing off to sleep, the Amban appeared in my room with a troop of Lamas at his heels. He came to say that they would not agree to our halting for one day even, and that we were to leave with the earliest signs of daybreak. I told them that it had been arranged that we were to halt for one day, and I was not going to change it now. They then waxed insolent, and one of them, a particularly militant dignitary of the Church, sprang to the front, and shaking his fist, said, "I told you that we had 3000 men with guns; they will be here in the morning, and if you are not out of this by then, you will see what will happen." I replied that we had thirteen English guns (as a matter of fact we had only five, but it was a game of bluff), and if the 3000 men came they would certainly be surprised at the reception they would receive. At the same time I collared a gun; a caravan driver near the door seized another; and though I knew him to be an arrant coward, on that occasion he played up properly, shouting out, "If it is going to be fighting, we had better begin at once."

The Amban got terribly excited, endeavouring to play the peacemaker; as both parties were only bluffing, it was not a very difficult task.

The halt was agreed to, and the disturbers of my rest departed.

The position of the Chinese in these parts seems very peculiar. What the status of the Amban is it is impossible to make out; he is treated with great respect so far as we saw, but possibly a good deal of the bowing and scraping that went on was for our benefit, in order that the Lamas, while twisting and turning him as it suited their purpose, might still keep up the farce that they were in every way subservient to the representative of a great power.

That the Chinese have got a pretty good foothold in Chiamdo was plainly demonstrated by the enormous numbers of them to be seen gazing at us as we rode past the town. There is no doubt that the Chinese in all parts of the world have a wonderful gift for ousting the natives from whatever country they get a footing in. The same thing has happened in Chinese Turkistan, Tibet, and California, and would most probably have happened in Australia had not legislation stepped in. With their industrious and economical habits, and constantly being reinforced by a steady stream of immigrants from the Celestial Empire, their foothold in a country grows steadily, until some day the people, exasperated by finding the benefits of their country monopolised by a race they dislike and despise (for a dislike of the Chinese is very general amongst all people thrown in contact with them), and also, though to a very much smaller extent, animated by disgust for their immoral habits and petty thefts, rise and clear the country. For a brief space the place is free of them; then once more they begin to come in by driblets, and the whole story is re-enacted. Such is the history of the Chinese in more countries than one; if no general massacre of them takes place, they can eat up a people against whom they would not stand for a moment in the open field—*vide* the history of the Mongols, the last chapters of which are now being enacted.

1st January 1892, Camp 128; 11,836 feet.—New Year's Day. A very long way from home and friends, but a great day for us, as the Lamas brought over a quantity of things to sell, consisting of sugar, tobacco, tea, raisins, flour, honey, and some mysterious dried Chinese fruits.

The Amban came over with the Lamas in order, as he said, to settle any disagreements that might arise in regard to the prices to be paid. However, there was no need for his intervention, as the prices asked for everything, with the exception of the sugar, were decidedly moderate, and in such an out-of-the-way place one could not expect to get sugar cheap. It was a great haul for us, as we had been for a long time strangers to anything in the way of luxury. We were particularly appreciative of the flour, as tsampa, a thing one gets terribly tired of, had been the staple article of our diet for so long.

After they had departed a message came from the Amban to ask if I would sell him any gold coins of the same pattern as one I had given him. I replied that I regretted exceedingly not being able to oblige him, as I had very few left, and wanted them to give to people who might give assistance farther on. He was not in the slightest discouraged, but sent another man with fifteen rupees to get one. As they had cost twenty-four rupees each, I did not feel much inclined to give them for less, and told the messenger so; after that he stopped his solicitations, and I heard nothing more about the matter. A poor mendicant monk, who had accompanied us for several marches, promised to come to our quarters after dark, and tell us whether we were being shown the right road. He kept his promise, and when he came said the road we were being shown was the best one to Bathang. I was very pleased to hear it, as I considered that the Lamas would certainly show us the road that it suited them best that we should take, utterly regardless of where it led to or what sort of travelling it was. I gave the informant a present of our sole remaining donkey. Poor beast, he had been marched off his legs, but had done us right royal service, and it was like parting with an old friend. Like most of his race he was full of character, and the way he used to come strolling into camp towards dark and take up his position close to the tent after the fate that befell his brethren (who, straying to some distance at night, had been snapped up by wolves), was a proof, if any was wanted, that the donkey is one of the most intelligent of animals, and infinitely the superior in that respect of the horse.

On the top of our house there was a sort of open courtyard-like place with sheds all round, used for storing chopped straw—a very common arrangement in Tibetan houses. I thought it a good plan to utilise this place in order to take observations for latitude, as it was well screened from view, and I knew that the sight of a theodolite and a bull's-eye lantern would most assuredly have aroused the superstitious fears of the people. Some one, however, must have been watching, as while engaged at it several stones and clods of earth were thrown at me. I immediately sent a man over to ask the head Lama what was the meaning of this interruption in my devotions in honour of the New Year. The answer was that he much regretted that I had been interfered with, and if the culprit could be caught he should be promptly flogged in my presence. Not content with sending the message by one of our men, he sent one of his own afterwards to repeat it, with the addition that to prevent my being annoyed again he had had all the inhabitants locked up for the night,—an extreme measure which I hardly expected him to take.

2nd January, Camp 129; 33 miles, 12,900 feet, Pandesar.—At daybreak, a Tibetan woman was seen outside our quarters lighting a fire in a furnace-like arrangement on the roof. We watched her with much interest; first of all she got a good bright fire, then she put in some twigs which gave out an enormous volume of smoke, and on the top she poured a lot of grain and a little water. We were told it was a sort of votive offering to the ancestral *manes.*

Just as we were finishing our breakfast the Lamas arrived to say good-bye. We seated them on boxes all round the room, and a desultory conversation of an exceedingly polite description was started. Suddenly they all rose, and making an obeisance in Chinese fashion, said that the head of the monastery sent his compliments and wanted a reward for the assistance given. It was rather difficult to see what assistance had been given, as the clerical community had done all they could to be obstructive. The bellicose gentleman who had threatened us with 3000 musketeers looked rather out of place soliciting bak-sheesh, and I did not at first feel much inclined to give any, but thinking it over I came to the conclusion that it would be advisable to get their good-will. Nothing can be done in Tibet except through the monks' assistance, so I gave them some silver and a gold coin for the head monk. Of course, they made it out that they had supplied the chopped straw that had been provided for our horses, and that they were the people who ought to receive payment; but I knew well that of whatever was given to them not a sou would find its way into the pockets of the unfortunate peasants from whom the things had been requisitioned. I always found out, whenever it was feasible, who had really supplied anything, and rewarded them separately, as I did on this occasion.

As regards transport, the custom of Tibet is that

the people living along the road to China are bound to supply travellers with carriage to the next place where animals are procurable. I presume they receive some sort of compensation in the way of immunity from taxes, but however that may be, I always distributed some money amongst the men who came with the animals. On discharging them this liberality on my part used to astonish them tremendously, and called forth a deal of bowing and a great show of tongues. It was quite a pleasure giving them anything and watching the delight they evinced.

After our clerical friends had received their money, we mounted and started. The road ran up a valley to a pass which was a good stiffish pull. All the way up enormous quantities of game were to be seen—musk-deer, partridges, and pheasants; the latter were of a kind new to us, something resembling grouse, but with a tuft on the head and some white in the tail. I should much have liked to have shot a couple, but all the valley is under the jurisdiction of the monks, who strongly object to shooting, and as it was as well to keep on good terms with them, I abstained.

After crossing the pass, we descended to a village where we had tea and changed animals. For some inexplicable reason, on this side the country is quite devoid of trees, though the soil and general appearance of the hills are much the same as on the other side, which is well wooded. Of course every one who has ever been in the Himalayas knows that the northern side of hills is often wooded, and the southern bare; but in this case our course lay east, up one valley and down another.

Our things did not arrive till after dark, but Dr. Thorold and myself posted on ahead, and on arrival at a sort of Chinese serai were ushered into a room, and tea and a fire in an iron basin were brought in; the fire was made of twigs that give a cheerful blaze and no smoke, the latter a great advantage in a country where the houses are not generally provided with chimneys or even with holes in the roof; but the twigs burn away so quickly that a man has always to be in attendance feeding the flame.

TIBETAN BLOOD PHEASANT (*ITHAGINIS GEOFFROYI*). See pages 297, 298.

CHAPTER XII

CHIAMDO TO GARTHOK

3rd January 1892, Camp 130 ; 28 miles, 12,400 feet, Tyat Bagang.—Another pass with a very long ascent; it seemed as if we were never going to reach the top. Though only 15,025 feet high, it took us four hours to get up. On the road we saw a couple of burhel absurdly tame, like all the animals about here. The descent was easy, and when we neared the foot, we halted, lit a fire, and had tea. While we were at tea our baggage came up, and I was much grieved to hear that a fine mule that had come all the way from Leh and one that any mountain battery might be proud of, had knocked up and been abandoned.

As we approached Tyat Bagang we were met by four Chinamen, who escorted us in. At every stage on this road a small party of Chinamen is quartered; two of them always escort any traveller of importance to the next stage and are there relieved. We always found them civil and inclined to give trustworthy information about the roads, etc., and though no doubt they knew that they would be well rewarded,

A TYPICAL TIBETAN TOWN—TYAT CHAMDI.

the way they always promptly produced tea and some little delicacies when we arrived tired and hungry at their station was very pleasing. I believe they are all soldiers, but I failed to find anything about them that could be connected with the profession of arms.

It is sometimes very hard to make out who are under China and who are under Lhasa. The place we left in the morning was most assuredly under the Deva Zhung, but as regards this place opinions are divided. The truth, I fancy, is that the people who bear a bad name for lawlessness and thieving say they are under whoever it suits them to be under for the time being, and at the same time take good care to pay taxes to neither, while both Governments, being weak in these parts, are unable to coerce them; so the good people of Tyat remain a puzzle to geographers.

4th January, Camp 131; Wamkha, 13 miles, 12,225 feet.—An easy march down a valley in which there was a great deal of cultivation and many villages. The hills were gaily decorated with flags in long rows. I thought it must be in honour of some festival, but was told it was not so, they were always there.

On approaching the village the Chinamen on the lines of communication were all out to usher us into the rest-house, a poor dilapidated building. Soon after we had got in, the headman of the village brought a scarf of welcome and some supplies, and was followed by a Lama who also brought a scarf, but in addition, instead of the useful supplies a rather mangy fox-skin. They both were well rewarded, the result being that nearly all the villagers turned up, bringing offerings of all sorts of articles for which we could have no possible use. I would not take any more, the mangy fox-skin was as much as any one could reasonably be expected to stand. They were as importunate in their endeavours to induce me to take them as they afterwards would have been in soliciting baksheesh had I accepted.

5th January, Camp 132.—The Tibetans who were supplying us with transport did not bring their animals till very late, the result being that we only did half the march we had intended to do. We crossed a pass as usual. The worst of this marching is that though the actual mileage covered each day is pretty large the geographical progress is extremely small, as it is always a case of zigzagging up one side of a pass and down the other.

At this stage some of the natives showed a talent which we had found very general throughout the country; it consisted of hiding some article belonging to us and after a great search producing it and claiming a reward. One gentleman was caught hiding my whip. Though they are less civilised, there are some talents which are very nearly as well developed in the Tibetan as the Chinaman.

6th January, Camp 133; 6 miles, 13,025 feet, Gamdi.—This was the place we should have reached the previous day. It is a large village with a Chinese rest-house and a Chinese official of sorts; but his position must be a very anomalous one, as he said the people were a turbulent thieving lot and owned allegiance to neither China nor Lhasa, and the only work he can have to do being to keep an eye on the line of communications.

The houses are of a pattern very common over a considerable stretch of country; they are rectangular and three-storied, the inside is open to the sky in the centre, the ground floor is used for the horses and cattle, the next has round the wall sheds for storing straw, etc.; above that there are dwelling-places also, of course, round the sides, there are no windows on the outside, which presents a sheer wall to the view from any direction. Similar or nearly similar pattern houses are to be found in many places besides Tibet where there is much fear of robbers—the pattern of house built being often a very fair guide to the social condition of a country.

7th January, Camp 134; 29 miles, 12,125 feet, Tyat Chamdi.—After crossing the Gam La we descended to a village where we changed baggage animals, but it took some time to collect them. We then continued our journey, but owing to the delay we did not reach Tyat Chamdi, which is a very large village, until after dark. On arriving we were taken to a miserable hovel, and told it was the rest-house; but anticipating that owing to the lateness of our arrival it would be impossible to get fresh transport on in the morning and that a day's halt would be imperative, we asked if no better quarters were available. They then showed us a place next door which was full of Chinamen; it looked a comfortable place, but just as we were beginning to unload the animals, we discovered that it was not a rest-house but a private one. I therefore sent to the headman and the Chinese mandarin to ask where we were to go, but the messengers came back saying the mandarin was in bed and would not be disturbed, and the headman, who was drunk, had refused to see them, but had hiccuped through the door that he would see us far enough before we got any assistance from him. However, the Amban's interpreter came down almost immediately afterwards to say that four small houses in the city were at our disposal. I went to see them, and was shown into a filthy opium den in a crowded part of the town, where there was no accommodation for our horses; so I returned to the Chinamen's house and made an arrangement with them to put up in it. By this time it was getting very late, and before we got anything to eat it was midnight.

In the morning with the very earliest streak of dawn a crowd had gathered to gaze at us, amongst whom a great number of Lamas of inferior rank; a miserable ruffian-like looking lot, the higher dignitaries of the Buddhist Church seeming to monopolise the food, clothes, and intellect. As, instead of being in a closed room, we were in a sort of open upstairs verandah, they were able to gratify their curiosity to the utmost. There they remained all day gazing for hours together with rapt attention at our every movement; those who had come early and secured good seats evidently considering themselves fortunate. From our quarters a very fair view of the place was obtained; it quite rises to the dignity of a small town, and contains a large monastery. The houses, as at Chiamdo, are flat-roofed and whitewashed.

About 10 A.M. three headmen arrived to say that transport animals were ready, and requested that we would move on at once. I said I wanted grain for my horses and tsampa for my men, and though willing to pay a fair price, I should not move till I got them. They departed to get the articles, and returned some time after midday, bringing in addition a bag of fine flour and two dried sheep. They then repeated their request that we would leave at once, as they said the people were a dangerous lot and they feared trouble if we remained. Though I certainly had no wish to linger, at the same time I judged it to be too late to start. The loading up always took a long time and the days were very short, so the chances were that we should have been benighted on the road. This would have stopped all mapping work; and apart from that, arriving at a place after dark was always very disagreeable. Fuel as a rule was only got with difficulty, and we ran the chance of going supperless to bed; so I declined to move, but said that if the animals were ready, we would start at daybreak. Of course they tried to make it out that we should arrive long before dark, if we started at once, but by this time I had quite given up putting any trust whatever in a Tibetan's word. The curiosity we excited was becoming a great nuisance as the country became more populous, so we decided to get some Chinese garments, not as a disguise, because I don't think any of the party would have passed muster as Chinamen, but simply in order that our appearance might excite less curiosity.

In Eastern Tibet Buddhism seems much more deeply impregnated with Hinduism than in Ladakh. On the stones composing Mānés,[1] figures of Hindu gods are often seen, and in one house I saw a brass image of Ganesha.

The people are great hands at pilfering. While our dinner was being prepared, the cook happened to take his eyes for a minute off a bag containing ginger which we had bought a few stages back, and it was promptly stolen. A crowd of people, mostly Lamas, were standing about, and I was strongly inclined to suspect one of the monks. They are most certainly quite capable of it.

At night I wanted to take observations for position, but the crowd were determined to stay all night. Those that had been lucky enough to secure seats were determined to hold on to them in order to get a good view of us when day broke, and as I did not want to have a row, I abstained.

9th January, Camp 135; 13 miles, 12,625 feet,

[1] See note, page 8.

Garing Doba.—As we opened our eyes in the morning there were the same people gazing at us, apparently never having taken their eyes off all night. The operation of dressing was watched with breathless interest; the idea of removing any garment to go to bed was quite novel, and as it involved putting them on again in the morning, it must have appeared to them a ridiculous waste of energy. We thought the same when we were up on the cold wind-swept Chang, but now the weather was getting mild, customs changed. Before leaving we had to find out who had supplied anything in order to reward them, but it was rather a difficult matter, as every man present in the crowd came forward and stated that he was the one and only man who had done anything for us, or given us anything. The more respectably-dressed of them far exceeded the others in the loudness of their clamourings for baksheesh. To the headman who had brought the supplies I gave something rather greater than the estimated value, and took no notice of men who had not been present when they were handed over; though I have no doubt that the headman had taken them from somebody in the town, and would not part with a cent of what he received from me. Still, with a couple of hundred claimants, it was impossible to adjudge to whom payment was due. This paying out of money for things received had quite upset the whole traditions of the town.

After loading up and making the best of our way

through the mob, we went up a valley in which there was a village where we had the option of staying for the night, or changing animals and going on. As they told us if we went on we could not reach the next stage before dark, we decided to halt.

The headman asked one of the caravan drivers of what religion we were. The caravan driver, a man of considerable fluency, said "Buddhists," to which the headman answered that he was very glad of it, as the only comfortable place in the village to put up in was the idol-house, but that the idol was a particularly touchy one, and if any one other than a pious Buddhist was allowed to enter his house, he would severely punish the village; but as we were Buddhists of course there would be no objection to our going there. This passing as Buddhists put an idea into my head. The last essay at taking observations by stealth had been a distinct failure, as evinced by the stones and clods of earth alighting round me during the operation, so I determined now to adopt new tactics. Sending for the headman I announced my intention of saying my devotions that evening according to the proper Buddhist ritual. Then, when evening came, having got all the paraphernalia out—a Buddhist bell, a dorji, a theodolite, a bull's-eye lantern, etc. — the service began. The caravan drivers, Mohammedans only partially acquainted with the religion they had adopted for the time being, rang the bell at intervals and chanted, "Om mani padmi hum,"[1] but the Mussulman Chinaman we had picked up at Tsuk Sun Dong Gong was quite an artist at it, bustling about lighting fires, and chanting what might be High Mass. The sub-surveyor, who was a Hindoo, brought the bull's-eye lantern to bear on the theodolite at the proper times, and looking through I fixed the star. Thus was the position of Garing Doba ascertained, and an odour of sanctity spread round me which lasted until a country more thickly populated with the heretical Chinese was reached.

BUDDHIST BELL AND DORJI.

A man hopelessly blind came to our quarters to be doctored, and on being told his case was hopeless he stayed to beg. That is a very favourite plan with the Tibetans. They come for medical treatment, and having received the best available, they refuse to move until money is also given them. I should not be inclined to recommend Tibet to members of the Faculty in search of a lucrative field for the exercise of their talents.

10th January, Camp 136; 35 miles, 13,325 feet, Achowa.—A very long march crossing two passes on the road, the country being of quite a different character from any we had seen for some time. It consisted of rolling, grassy, treeless hills of the same

[1] "Oh! the flower in the lotus leaf, oh!"

nature as those on the Chang, and goa were to be seen. Our things, or at least those of them that were on yaks, did not arrive until 11 P.M. Our cooking things were on a pony, and got in about 8.30 P.M., but it did not really much matter when they got in, as the Chinamen in charge of the *toongshang* or rest-house gave us a repast, consisting of fish which was excellent, some mutton, which also was very good, and two indescribable dishes that, tasting once, we did not care to try again. None of the *toongshangs* on this road are very palatial, but this one was dilapidated to a marvellous extent.

January 11th, Camp 137 ; 20 miles, 13,425 feet, Asi. — Before starting we were told that it was necessary to take an armed escort, as all this Chang-like country forms a sort of Alsatia, to which Tibetans, who have made their homes too hot to hold them, flock. There they bid defiance to both China and Lhasa, and carry on a flourishing business in the Chukpa line. This march between Achowa and Asi is said to contain their favourite spots for lying in wait for caravans, so we marched accompanied by ten matchlock-men whom the headman of Achowa insisted on giving us, though I did not think it at all necessary. Chukpas are very different men from what I take them to be if they would attack by daylight a caravan in which there were breech-loaders.

From the top of a pass we crossed the same sort of Chang-like country, which could be seen stretching away to the north and east as far as the eye could reach, while in the foreground several herds of goa were grazing.

On the road one of the Tibetans told a caravan driver that he had heard the English were going to take the country, and that he was very pleased at it, and nearly all the people would be so. On being asked why, he said that he had heard that the English were very rich, and never took anything by force, but paid highly for everything. I have often heard the same argument from people in other Asiatic countries. Patriotism may almost be said to be non-existent.

A great many of the inhabitants of these parts fought against us in Sikkim. Their recollections of the effect of the fire of breech-loaders are most lively. One man, who had a scar on his face, related his experience to me; he said: "I was told I had to go and fight the English, and with a lot of others I started for Sikkim. When we got there we suddenly heard a rattle of musketry; a great many men fell. I got hit in the face, turned round and went straight for home, and have stayed there since." He was in no way animated with a wish to die a soldier's death.

This place belongs to the Deva Zhung, and the headman who came to see us said that unless we had a passport from Lhasa we could not be allowed to proceed. Suspecting that all he wanted was to create difficulties in order to obtain a bribe, and knowing well that he would be very glad to get us out of the country, I told him nothing would suit us better than a halt, and if we halted for a month our own ponies would recover sufficiently to allow us to be independent as regards carriage of anybody. Transport promptly arrived with a request that we would go on.

January 12th, Camp 138 ; Rashwa.—A long march crossing three easy passes *en route*, on the tops of which men were stationed, keeping a look-out for Chukpas ; they are kept watching there day and night. The stronghold of these brigands is said to be fifteen marches off and a place of great natural strength. Some time ago a thousand men from Chiamdo went against it, but the Chukpas, rolling stones down on their assailants, killed two hundred and caused the rest to flee ; since that they have been left alone. The people here say that the Chinese on the lines of communication are supported from China, and they are not obliged to give them anything except on payment ; the only things they are obliged to supply free are wood, fodder, and transport to travellers of rank.

January 13th, Camp 139 ; 26 miles, 13,700 feet, Mongothong.—Up a pass 15,100 feet high, with numbers of white pheasants to be seen (of which we shot a couple) running about in every direction, and then over an uninhabited country with rounded hills to a *toongshang* standing alone in a valley.

Goa were plentiful and marks of the *Shoa-u-chu* stag were to be seen.

January 14th; 19 miles, 12,991 feet, Monkong or Garthok.—As we marched down a valley the character of the country gradually changed, becoming more wooded, and at Monkong cultivation was reached. Outside the village a crowd of people were collected to gaze at us; they followed to the *toongshang*, but when we entered, the Chinaman in charge shut the doors and kept them out, so we were left inside in comparative peace. This is the place at which M. Bonvalôt, who passed to the north of Chiamdo and then came south by a route lying to the east of ours, joined the Bathang road; it is a largish village, and amongst the inhabitants there are said to be two hundred and fifty Chinese. As the road to Ta Chen Lu had been previously explored, I made inquiries about a direct route to Tonquin or into Burma, but eventually took the Ta Chen Lu road. This I did because I heard that there were two hundred Europeans there and I wanted to see them, and partly because on the other routes it would have been necessary to have our own transport, as it was impossible to hire, and it would have taken a very long time to equip a caravan here; the officials also were very anxious to hurry us on.

It was very comfortable getting into these Chinese rest-houses after a long experience of tent-life on the Chang; but there is one great drawback about them, and that is the want of fireplaces and chimneys, a trayful of charcoal being a poor substitute for a roaring wood fire. The Chinese seem to have a powerful objection to chimneys. In Turkistan the rest-houses are built on the same pattern, and, travelling in winter, I found it advisable to put up either in the mud huts intended for servants or else in the private house of some Turki, in preference to the well-built and handsome but cellar-like rest-house.

The head Chinaman here had been to Darjiling, and he never failed to bring in the name of Darjiling in his endeavours to enlighten me as to the geography of the country ahead. For instance, he said that after passing Ta Chen Lu, if we kept straight on we should reach Shanghai, at which place we should find the Darjiling road. Tonquin and Canton were also described as places whence roads run to Darjiling.

He asked to see our passport and I showed it with much trepidation, fearing that when it was seen that it was for Turkistan he would create difficulties, but he did not. He seemed much impressed with the signatures of the high subscribing parties thereto, and promised to send information of its contents to the mandarin at Bathang. We halted for a day here, and spent it skinning pheasants and having a general wash up. In Tibet one's views get very much modified as to the proper interval to be observed between tubs, and there is no doubt that in extreme cold, when doing hard work, tubbing is a mistake—it seems to take too much out of one.

ON THE ROOF OF A HOUSE—EASTERN TIBET.

CHAPTER XIII

GARTHOK TO LITHANG

16th January; 18 miles, 12,420 feet, Phula.— A very easy march down a lovely valley. The more one sees of Eastern Tibet, the more one is impressed with its beauty, particularly of those parts under Lhasa; those under China as a rule are rather inferior. A sort of minor dignitary accompanied us on the road; he was drunk and most persistent in his solicitations for *Sori* as it is called in Tibetan, baksheesh in well-nigh every other language; giving him some to go away was of absolutely no avail, he stuck to us like a limpet. A peculiarity in the character of the people of Tibet is that, whereas in most countries only the poor people solicit baksheesh, in Tibet those comparatively well off are the most troublesome; they are again out-classed altogether by the monks.

When we reached the rest-house, the Chinaman in charge had a repast ready for us, as was almost invariably the case. It was very curious to notice the number of dishes in which ingredients that had been brought all the way from China were used.

They were particularly strong in a kind of dried sea-weed-like stuff that was decidedly eatable. The Chinese seem to be as fond of carrying about their national luxuries with them as we are of tinned foods, sauces, pickles, etc. On this road one could very easily travel with nothing but a roll of bedding; tents are quite superfluous, and cooking things might be dispensed with.

On the wall of the rest-house a Mohammedan, probably a native of India, had written his name Moonshi Mahomed in the Persian character.

17th January; 26 miles, Lande.—Over three small passes, the hills beautifully wooded all the way. From between the last two a dazzling snowy range was showing up against the blue sky; to the south of it is a place called Sakha, the generic name for every place whence salt is brought. The Tibetans said that there were two Europeans living there, and spoke most kindly of them; afterwards we learned that they were French Catholic missionaries, people of whom, so far as my limited experience goes, it is impossible to speak otherwise. We met at the rest-house a very poor, wayworn-looking youth, who said he was going on a pilgrimage to Lhasa, and had been eight months coming from Canton on foot.

18th January; 10 miles, Bon.—At this place there was no *toongshang* or rest-house, so we put up in the headman's house; he was very civil, and gave us a repast on arrival. His wife, a motherly-looking soul, who brought the dishes to the door of the room, evidently washed her face; it was quite respectably clean.

19th January, 13½ miles, Khonjika.—An easy march, the greater part of which was down a well-wooded narrow valley. On the road we changed animals three times—rather a ridiculous proceeding considering the shortness of the march. As we should soon be getting into a low-lying hot country, and as Ladakhis always get ill in countries lower than their own high cold regions, I suggested to the caravan drivers that it would be a good plan if they returned to their homes *via* Lhasa, where all had friends and relations. I offered them pay in advance and subsistence allowance for five months, but they did not care about it; they said if it was my order they would go, but they would prefer to stay with me until India was reached. Of course I had no intention or wish to give them an order. My only idea was to let them decide themselves, but that is often a difficult thing to get people in the East to understand — they always want an order. In this case, as I saw they would rather come on with me, I agreed to their doing so. Their aversion to the Lhasa route was partly fear of being attacked by Chukpas on the road, and partly fear that the Lhasa people would punish them for bringing Europeans into the country.

20th January.—The Khonji La pass, near which we were, was ridiculously easy, and in no way deserving of being dignified with the name of a pass.

The descent to the Di Chu river was down a narrow valley; near the top it was wooded, and on the trees squirrels were to be seen. On reaching the village of Tangati, where we changed animals, the trees had been left behind, and we found ourselves in a country of scrub-covered hills, with patches of cultivation here and there. The whole place had a spring-like appearance, and the barley in the fields was sprouting —a great change, as two days back we had been apparently in midwinter. After the great cold we had been accustomed to, it seemed very hot indeed; according to the inhabitants it is never cold, and snow only rarely falls.

The Di Chu is a fine big stream, with clear water. Here and there are rapids, which is a great pity, as otherwise it would be navigable for large boats, and a very interesting journey might be made down it. As it is, nothing could live in the rapids as we saw them, but possibly at certain times of the year they may be passable. The river is crossed by a ferry: the people said that for very many years the advisability of constructing a bridge had been under discussion, but nothing had been done. A couple of men sent by the mandarin at Bathang met us on the road, an unexpected honour that led us to believe we should find him agreeable and friendly.

21st January.—Owing to a late start we were unable to reach Bathang as we had hoped to do. We passed through a very uninteresting country, quite different from what we had been accustomed to ever since leaving Chiamdo; bare, scrubby, dried-up looking, rounded hills had taken the place of the pine-clad valleys backed with snowy peaks.

22nd January; 8500 feet, Bathang.—Continuing up the same valley to Bathang, a large monastery

CHARACTERS ON CHINESE VISITING CARD.[1]

with gilded minarets came in view. On approaching nearer, the place was found to consist of three parts: the monastery and its adjuncts; the Chinese town; and

[1] These characters representing my name were reproduced from my Chinese "visiting card"—a strip of flimsy scarlet paper some 10 inches long by 4½ wide.

the Tibetan town, a miserable-looking collection of huts on the other side of the river, connected with the other two parts by a bridge. When we arrived we went to the Chinese town, and were shown into a rather pretentious Chinese building made entirely of wood; on the walls strips of red paper with Chinese writing were pasted up, and on the gate was the representation of a dragon. A crowd of people followed us through the streets and into our quarters; but some Chinamen, with bamboos of the kind usually used in China for flogging criminals, cleared the courtyard, and we were left in peace. It is not often that the Chinese authorities take such care for the protection or comfort of travellers, and the only way I can account for it is, that they thought we were a pretty strong party, and wished to keep on good terms with us. This is the first place, coming from the east, at which any signs of Chinese authority are seen; but even here the Chinese are either inimical to Europeans, or else their power is only nominal, as the history of the French mission station that was established here for some years, and wrecked and pillaged by the mob in 1887, amply proves. The Chinese authorities professed friendliness all the time, only regretting inability to restrain the people, the old story that European representatives listen to in all gravity. The Tsungli yamen, of course, promised compensation, and that passports would be granted, authorising the re-establishment of the mission. By the Treaty of Tien Tsin the establishment of mission stations is specially provided for; but nothing has been done, and the missionaries at Ta Chen Lu are still in communication with the authorities, in hopes of returning to a place where they owned land and houses, now gutted.

We had a little difficulty at first about getting supplies; no one seemed inclined to sell anything, and as I also wanted to make arrangements for transport, I sent to the yamen in order to open up communication with the mandarin. Unfortunately he was not capable of giving much assistance as he was drunk, and on an attendant's endeavouring to waken him, he turned round and spat in his face, and then murmuring something, described by my messenger as being more or less of a stern, uncompromising, and even defiant nature, he became unconscious once more. However, the Tibetan gamboo shortly afterwards came to our quarters, bringing supplies. The prices asked were rather high; suttoo (tsampa) about 12 lbs. for a rupee, rice about 10 lbs., fine flour about 8 lbs., not really exorbitant rates, but still, no doubt, considerably above market prices. Rupees circulate freely, being the coin in general use, but there are no Indian small coins; so the difficulty is got over by cutting rupees into halves and quarters.

The morning after arrival, in order to have a walk, I went out very early; later in the day it would have been impossible, or at least exceedingly disagreeable, as the people were thoroughly Chinese.

I strolled towards the monastery which, together with all the buildings connected with it, is enclosed within a high wall, presenting rather a fort-like appearance. From a distance of a couple of hundred yards or so, I noticed that the gates were open; but, as I approached, they were hastily shut in my face. The Lamas are terribly afraid of any one seeing the inside of their monasteries, and the riches contained in them.

25th January; 23 miles, Pongotomo.—Up a valley with precipitous sides the whole way; the upper part was well clothed with firs and a species of tree something like holly oak, which were covered with a moss-like creeper.

Pongotomo is a most dilapidated-looking village, situated in a small clearing in the forest, in which there are some small patches of cultivation. The rest-house is on a par with the remainder of the village, and supplies were scarce and dear.

26th January; 17 miles, 13,145 feet, Tashu.—Over a stony but not very difficult pass on which snow was lying. Descending, we got clear of the snow before reaching Tashu; but no sooner had we got under cover than it came down heavily. The village is a very poor place, built entirely of wood.

Supplies were very dear; one rupee was asked for a fowl, whereas in Bathang four annas is the ordinary price. I tried hard to buy a sheep, but whenever a price was agreed to, the Tibetans promptly went back on their word, and refused to part with it. They are extremely hard people to deal with, as they are not only grasping but shifty; for example, a man asks a certain price for a thing, and after much talk he agrees to take, say, five rupees; when you think the affair is settled, and begin to count out the money, he promptly swears eight rupees was the price agreed to. The fact of the matter is, that your having consented to give five rupees, whereas the real price is probably two rupees, has demoralised him, by opening to his vision dreams of boundless wealth.

The women here had their hair done in a fashion we had not seen before. From the centre of the forehead it was brought down to the end of the nose, and cut off square there. It was something like a miniature horse's tail, stuck on where the parting would be in the European fashion.

27th January; 24 miles, Rathi.—Through alpine scenery over the Rathi La. The top of the pass is well above the forest line, and there a herd of burhel was seen. Rathi is a village of even a meaner character than Tashu, and it was almost impossible to purchase anything; no sheep were procurable, but we managed to get some mutton for ourselves; the Mohammedan followers of course would not touch it, as it had been killed by a Buddhist. As regards grass, we were regularly boycotted, a rupee being asked for nine small wisps of which a pony could easily eat twenty; but as the hills were covered with it, I preferred to turn them out to forage for themselves. There is no *toongshang* here, but a broken hut is placed at the disposal of travellers, which had one immense advantage, viz. a hole in the roof which allowed the smoke, or at least a portion of it, to escape.

28th January; 19 miles, 12,793 feet, Namda.—Another dilapidated village. The road ran down a valley which is the favourite winter quarters of the neighbouring nomads; their black tents were to be seen in all the side valleys, and the hills were covered with herds of yak and sheep. On the road we bought a very fair sheep for one rupee eight annas, which was cheap enough. We passed a high stone tower-like building of a type very superior to anything ordinarily seen in these regions, but uninhabited and falling into ruins. The natives say that very long ago it was built by a king who ruled in these parts, for a favourite wrestler called Too Tem Doom Boo.

In the rest-house, which was in a terrible state of dirt, an old woman and her daughter appeared to have taken up permanent quarters; they were very civil, and proceeded to sweep out the place and light a fire directly we arrived, but the price they asked for some grass they had for sale led me to think that the relative values of rupees and grass in Tibet must be founded on exaggerated impressions regarding the depreciation of silver.

29th January; 16 miles, 12,630 feet, Ramo.—After crossing a couple of very easy passes we descended into the valley in which Ramo is situated, where there are several other villages and some cultivation. The people have the reputation of being a very stiff-necked race, and the way they treated the two Chinese soldiers who were supposed to be our escort bore this out. At the first place at which they asked for quarters for the night, an old man struck one in the face and told them to be gone; the next place they tried they were spat at; after that they decided to go to a place five miles off, where one of their fellow-countrymen lived. To us, however, the people were civil enough, and we had no difficulty about getting quarters.

30th January; 21 miles, Zomda.—A good deal of the journey was over a treeless country with granitic boulders scattered about. We had hoped to have crossed the Gara La Pass, but by 4.30 P.M. we had only reached a little hut under the pass, inhabited by an old woman and a youth, an uninviting-looking spot—snow lying in patches, a cold wind and leaden sky—not a place to linger in; but it was too late to face the pass, so there was nothing to do but halt for the night.

31st January; 29 miles, Lithang.—As we had a long march with a pass in front of us, we got up very early, and having dressed by candle-light, started with the earliest streak of dawn. After crossing the pass we descended to a rest-house, where we stopped to have tea, and then resumed our journey. Soon afterwards the town of Lithang came in sight; it is situated at the foot of a range of hills, and a broad open valley runs across its front. From a little distance off it appears to be all monastery, and it certainly must contain an enormous number of monks.

As we approached, one of the Chinese soldiers of our escort bolted; knowing well the customs of Chinese escorts, I thought that pointed to the prospect of a row. The other Chinese soldier was furtively looking round him for an opportunity to follow his companion's example, so I had him watched, as we wanted a guide. The interpreter who had gone on in front came back reporting that he could not find the *toongshang*, and the people refused to direct him; this certainly did not look as if we were going to receive an enthusiastic welcome. On reaching the gates the Chinese soldier was put in front to show the way, and we entered in single file. Suddenly in a narrow part, slipping off his horse, he placed himself behind me, and I found myself in front of some infuriated Tibetans, who had big stones in their hands and were dancing about in a threatening manner. To the best of my ability I endeavoured, with the assistance of a caravan driver who was close behind, to explain that we only wanted to find the rest-house, and were peaceful travellers. Some Lamas who came along the street were appealed to, but they only hurried on the faster, and the men with the stones, gathering courage from my conciliatory tone, grew fiercer and fiercer and advanced to within a few paces.

Thinking things were getting serious, I drew my carbine and rammed a cartridge in, with the effect of making the men who had threatened us vanish up an alley. The Chinese who were lingering on their door-steps, gazing at the scene, disappeared inside, slamming the doors after them, and we were left in possession of the street; however, we were not much better off than before, as we were in a blind alley, and there was no one to direct us. The Chinese soldier who had guided us so far, and had slipped off his horse when things began to look awkward, had disappeared into a house, leaving his horse in the street. We therefore held a council of war, standing in the middle of an apparently deserted city, and came to the conclusion that, as we were in a *cul de sac*, the best thing to do would be to retreat. This we did, and after going about 200 yards, seemed to get into a region where the action of loading the carbine had not been seen, as the Chinese came pouring out of their houses, and several of them offered us accommodation; but as none of them had any place in which the horses could be put, I was obliged to decline their offers, and got one of them to go to the yamen to ask the mandarin where we should go. He was a man that rather gave me a shock by addressing me in Hindustani, which he spoke fairly well, but he would no doubt have spoken it with more idiomatic correctness and less fluency had he been perfectly sober. As he had lived fourteen years in Darjiling he had had ample opportunities of picking up the language, and his anxiety to assist pointed to his having thoroughly understood the system on which sahibs pay for services received. He quickly went off to the yamen, and returned with permission for us to occupy a Chinese building, to which we were speedily conducted. As soon as we had settled down, an official came to ask for how long we intended to halt. I answered that we intended to proceed in the morning if we could get transport and enough food to carry us on to the next carry at which things were procurable. The official message and presently returned with a message from the Amban that he regretted that he could not treat us as guests ought to be treated; that he would have liked to have supplied us with everything free, but unfortunately he dared not do anything for fear of the Lamas. There was no doubt about it; his position was exactly the same as that of his compatriot at Chiamdo, viz. his presence tolerated, but his power *nil.* The Lamas are the rulers of the country, the people their bond-slaves, and the Chinese a stalking horse to be made use of in their relations with foreign powers.

CHAPTER XIV

LITHANG TO TA CHEN LU

1st February; 23 miles, Horchuka.—One of the things we had endeavoured to get was a man to bake bread enough to last us for three or four days. The mandarin said he would send us a man who would bake it overnight, but the man preferred to do it in the morning. While he was busy at it, a myrmidon came from the yamen to ask him why he had not obeyed the mandarin's orders and baked it the previous evening. The baker was not going to be intimidated by any one, and promptly caught up a stone. The myrmidon fled incontinently, leaving the man he had come to intimidate master of the field. In these parts the same respect for a limb of the law does not exist as in India.

Before we started, the Hindustani-speaking Chinaman turned up. I had made up my mind to enlist him as interpreter, but was disappointed to find that with returning sobriety his knowledge of the language had ebbed away, and he certainly did not know enough to make an efficient interpreter. About midday we started, our route lying over the same kind of country as before Lithang. Nomads' tents were to be seen in all the sheltered hollows, and herds were grazing in every direction. Down the bed of a stream whose course we followed, there were innumerable signs of gold-washing. One plan the natives had was new to me; it consisted first of all of a stream of water like a mill-lade detached from the main stream; towards the end, the water was concentrated into a narrow wood-lined channel, and then shot out with great force, striking a piece of peat-like turf. The soil, as excavated from the river bed, was thrown in at the head of the trough-like channel, and being carried down by the current, was thrown against the turf, and the gold stuck there, the rest of the soil being carried away by the water.

2nd February; 12,979 feet, 20 miles, Thamo Rothang.—Over a couple of very easy passes, the country generally of a Chang-like character until near the rest-house, where the sides of the valley became more precipitous, and trees appeared, amongst which white pheasants were to be seen in numbers. Thamo Rothang consists of nothing but a rest-house, and a few huts round it. The rest-house had a hole in the roof to let the smoke out, so it was comparatively comfortable. An attempt to sweep it out had also been made in our honour, but in true oriental fashion the dirt had simply been swept into a corner, while some pigs, disgusted at being evicted from their usual quarters, wandered disconsolately about the courtyard, making continual endeavours to get back again, only to be driven off by the execrations of our horrified Mussulmans, who were having their prejudices terribly shocked as we were getting into a country of Chinamen and their invariable attendants—pigs.

3rd February; *10½ miles, Galuk.*—Across a ridge and then down into a valley, in which there was a good deal of cultivation.

KOONON (*TETRAOPHASIS SZECHENYII*). See page 298.

4th February; *17 miles, Lanipa.*—After getting in, as three hours of daylight remained, we went to look for pheasants in jungle composed principally of a sort of holly oak with a few pine trees scattered about. We found three sorts: *Shagga* (Crossoptilon tibetanum; see pages 178, 295), *Tsiri* (Ithaginis geoffroyi; see pages 199, 297), and *Koonon* (Tetraophasis szechenyii; see page 298). All three sit on trees, but the *Koonon*, when hustled by a spaniel, takes boldly to the wing; while the *Tsiri*, a very mean bird, simply flies on to the nearest tree, and sits there in the most ridiculously tame manner; and when he does fly it is very feebly.

5th February; 24 miles, Nagchuka.—Over a very small pass, and then down a valley, in which some *koonon* were found sitting on the branches of trees. In shooting for specimens one does not stand much on ceremony, so going underneath, I knocked a couple off their perches—a male and female; unfortunately the male's tail was so knocked about that he was no good as a specimen. After securing them I followed the caravan, the road gradually getting rougher and the climate warmer. About three-quarters of the way down some monkeys were seen—sure sign of a change in the temperature. On the road I met a man riding, who promptly slipped off his horse, and kneeling down made obeisance by bumping his head several times on the ground. I felt much pleased and flattered, and began to think, in spite of the fact that one knee was sticking through my trousers, and the other was only prevented from doing so by a large leather patch, that there must be something very *distingué* in my appearance, as he evidently took me for, at least, a royal dignitary. However, when the gentleman attempted to rise it was evident that he was too drunk to do so without assistance, a fact which considerably discounted the value to be put upon his genuflections.

The Nag Chu, a river with a considerable volume

of water, is crossed by a bridge of boats close to Nagchuka, a very Chinese-looking village, situated on the left bank, and surrounded by precipitous mountains. The population, mostly Chinese, were all out to gaze at us, but we were pretty well used to being stared at as if we were some new sort of wild beast, and did not mind it as long as they did not take to throwing stones or other missiles.

We were shown into very comfortable quarters, and a man came from the mandarin with all sorts of civil messages and offers of assistance. Mandarin-like, he also regretted that owing to illness he was unable to call on us himself, as he would have liked to do.

Flour cost about a rupee for 18 lbs., and tsampa the same.

6th February; 29 miles, Uru Tonga.—A rather long march up a valley all the way, passing a high watch-tower where, according to orders, two men are always posted to keep a look-out for enemies; but as none live near or ever come that way by any chance, they naturally never see any. On the road we saw some *Shagga* at 9000 feet, the lowest point at which we had seen them.

The population of Uru Tonga is nearly entirely Chinese.

7th February; Maya Golok.—Hearing that there were two missionaries here, I pushed on in front of the caravan, anticipating with pleasure meeting once more with Europeans; but on arrival I was much disappointed to find that they were absent at Ta Chen Lu.

The people spoke most kindly of them, and they are evidently regarded both with affection and respect; their influence for good seemed to me most apparent as regards the children, who came up in a simple trustful way, quite different from the combination of fear and impudence one ordinarily meets with. As regards converting the people, I regret to say they have not been very successful. The only Christian in the place was one who was the sole and only man who stuck to his adopted religion after the *émeute* at Bathang. Tibet is not a good field for missionaries. With a similar people even under British rule, where they are naturally not in the hands of the Lamas as they are in Tibet, very little progress is made; as may be seen in the results of many years' work in Lahaul and Ladakh by the Moravian missionaries, against whom no one, not even the most anti-missionary sceptic, could say a word.

On the road an enormous quantity of tea was met with, being transported on mules and yaks from Ta Chen Lu to Lhasa; in fact, the whole of this road up to Ta Chen Lu was littered with animals carrying it, and beyond Ta Chen Lu well into Szechuen the string of coolies was incessant. The mules are of a good transport class, and sell for about fifty or sixty rupees.

In the evening we were treated to a Chinese

performance; it consisted of a huge dragon-like figure made of paper, inside which two men concealed themselves and jumped about, while the attendants beat cymbals; it was an entertainment apt to pall on one after a short time.

8th February; 15 miles, Amia To.—Woke up in the morning to find the ground covered with snow, which, however, quickly melted directly the sun rose.

The road lay along a valley in which numerous villages were scattered about; these villages are strongly built of stone, and as the houses are all joined together and several stories high, they present a very chateau-like appearance from a little distance off.

The house in which we put up contained innumerable prayer-wheels, showing that we were not yet clear of Tibet and its Buddhist observances. In the kitchen there was a fine big stove made of hardened clay, but without a chimney, and as a fire was burning, the atmosphere was very thick. Two travellers, a monk and a layman, seated on the floor, were being supplied by the guidwife with tea, tsampa, and meat; the latter, in accordance with a custom that obtains widely in Tibet, they ate raw.

At first we had great difficulty about getting supplies, the people refusing to give anything, but as we were out of tsampa, something had to be got. So I spoke rather sharply to the headman, the result being that things, the existence of which in the village five minutes before had been denied, were promptly produced, and the people were much astonished and delighted when I paid for them.

9th February, Chitu.—Crossed the Gi La pass; fairly easily. On the west side I was astonished to see a horseman in Chinese clothes, but with a decidedly European appearance, approaching. When he got near, the problem was solved by his salutation of *Bon jour, Monsieur.* He was one of the French missionaries, and it was a great pleasure meeting him. Unfortunately the place where we met was a bitterly cold spot, and the snow was coming down heavily, so we did not have as long a talk as we should have liked to have, but we heard from him that three of his countrymen were at Ta Chen Lu and that we should have the pleasure of meeting them next day.

All the day the snow continued falling heavily, and by the time we reached Chitu it was about a foot deep; it must have been much deeper on the higher ground. We were over the last of our Tibetan passes not an hour too soon.

10th February, 11 miles.—Ta Chen Lu, Gyatartse, Tarsedo, or Darchendo, as it is variously called. As the arranging for transport would take several days, Dr. Thorold decided to halt at Chitu and shoot for a few days; so I went on alone, trudging through snow for the first part; but lower down, as the sun came out, it melted quickly, and the streets of Ta Chen Lu were in a slippery state worthy of London at its worst.

A good house in the town, boasting a glass pane inserted in a window mostly of paper, was placed at our disposal; and the landlady, a worthy-looking woman, brought me some tea. After drinking it, I went off to call on the missionaries MM. Girandot and Mussot. I found them in what appeared to me very comfortable quarters, but I doubt if they would have seemed so to any one coming recently from civilisation. The few pictures and other evidences of refinement round them were very refreshing to see. The missionaries were dressed in Chinese clothes. One of my first questions was, "Any news from Europe?" There was nothing very exciting. The great powers were, as they had been for some years, keeping their armies up to concert pitch. They "make fearful musters and prepare defence," but the spark to set Europe in a blaze had not yet appeared.

In Asia there had been disturbances in the Yangtse valley, consisting, as they usually did, of attacks on inoffensive missionaries; and two Englishmen, seeing a mission station in flames and thinking the fire accidental, had gone to render assistance and been murdered by the mob. But the Chinese had made a show of repentance, and the European powers had professed themselves satisfied. The accounts of missionary work were not encouraging. The destruction of the mission station at Bathang had been a most serious blow, just when they were obtaining a footing and the confidence of the people. They complained most bitterly of the opposition of the

Lamas, and in echoing their words I am stating what I know of my own opinion to be the fact. These Lamas press with a heavy burden on the necks of the people, and the poor Tibetans, timid and superstitious, bear the yoke quietly, tilling their fields and tending their flocks that the monks may live at ease. Well do the Lamas know that a different state of affairs would be produced by contact with Europeans and the spread of the Gospel; therefore they judge, and that wisely from their point of view, that the best thing to do is to work up the people by appeals to their superstitions and threats of calamities to oppose the entry of foreigners.

I got most useful information from the missionaries regarding the route to Shanghai. To Yatu, on a tributary of the Yangtse, it was eight days, bad going most of the way. Coolies were mostly used, but the road was practicable for mules and ponies. From Yatu it was three days on a raft to Kiating, where boats were procurable, and from there it was all plain sailing to Ichang, where steamers were to be met with. In summer, however, when the snows are melting, that route becomes too dangerous to be practicable. I decided to take mule transport as far as Yatu, as travelling with coolies is terribly tedious work. By the aid of the assistance kindly rendered by the missionaries, I succeeded in making a contract at what no doubt was the proper rate. Had it not been for their presence my difficulties would undoubtedly have been much greater.

11th February.—Went for a stroll in the morning before breakfast, and after it busied myself overhauling our baggage. There were some things not worth taking any farther, such as the tents for instance.

In the afternoon I went for a walk through the town. The streets are very narrow, and crowded with Chinese shops. Matches, the pioneers of commerce, evidently form a staple article of trade.

12th and 13th February.—Changed some gold-dust for silver, getting in weight at the rate of 16½ for 1 of gold. No doubt as a stranger I was taken in, but I don't believe the proper rate is more than 17. Gold is still cheaper at Lithang, the rate being only 14 of silver to 1 of gold. I sold the remainder of my ponies to some Lamas; the holy men were very anxious that no one should know they had bought them, paying me the money when no one was present, and saying they would take them away in the night, as they wished to avoid paying a duty levied on all animals bought in the town.

Our landlord was a merchant, and said he had been twice to Calcutta *viâ* Lhasa, and had made a lot of money, particularly on musk. I suggested that the Bhamo route would be quicker, but he was afraid of the robbers on that road. Except the disturbed state of the country, I cannot see what hindrance there is to trade springing up on that route.

14th, 15th, and 16th February.—Dr. Thorold came

in on the 14th, having shot a female *Napi*, a sort of small chocolate-coloured deer (*Elaphodus cephalophus*). On the 16th he was down with fever, as also were two of the men. Ta Chen Lu is a very unhealthy place. The previous year there was hardly a family that did not lose a member, and hardly a soul in the place that was not down more or less with

PHASIANUS ELEGANS.

fever. In addition to being an unhealthy climate, it is also a very disagreeable one—damp, cold, and windy; when it is not raining it is snowing; altogether a most depressing place. That the missionaries stay there, shows what enthusiasm can induce men to do.

The only amenity I saw in the place was the pheasant (*Phasianus elegans*, see page 296) when shooting in the river bed. They are something like the English and Turkistan pheasants, and fairly numerous. With a couple of dogs good sport can be got, but unfortunately we ran out of cartridges.

On the 18th Thorold was still in bed, and I felt feverish, but we made up our minds to march next day if our temperatures were under 100°, and get out of the place. However in the morning both of us were a great deal too ill to rise, and we were not able to get up before the 24th, and then we were terribly weak, partly on account of the fever, which seemed of a very debilitating nature, and partly on account of some Chinese drugs we had taken.

Our intention had been to ride, but we were too weak, and so we decided to go in palanquins instead.

CHAPTER XV

THROUGH CHINA BACK TO INDIA

25th February, 20 miles, Irdosi.—We hoped to have left Ta Chen Lu early, but the contractor and his men were terribly dilatory, and we did not get away till well after midday.

The road, which was very bad, was quite crowded with coolies carrying tea for the Tibetan market. The loads were enormous, especially considering the very indifferent physique of the men carrying them. These coolies wear grass sandals of the kind known in the Himalayas as *phulas*. About 3.30 P.M. my men put me down and vanished into a tea-shop. For some time I sat still awaiting their lordships' pleasure; but at last, getting impatient, I got out of the palki and went to see what they were up to, when I found that one of them, having had an argument with the contractor, had walked off in dudgeon. As in my weak state I did not feel inclined to walk, I put the contractor between the shafts, and we started. Unfortunately he was more accustomed to smoking opium than working, so the result was that when night fell we were several miles from the halting-place. As they could not carry the palki in the dark, there was nothing to do then but get out and walk, which I did; but after falling twice from weakness, and realising the fact that the road in many places ran along the edge of cliffs which I might in the dark fall over at any moment, I made up my mind to sit down and wait for something to turn up. I had not sat long before some of our men, bringing with them a lamp, arrived, having come back to look for me, and within an hour I was in the tea-house at which we were to halt for the night.

These Chinese rest-houses are often very well built, made of wood, with large rooms, and showing good carpentry, but they are terribly odoriferous, the sanitary arrangements being infamous.

26th February, Lodinshoma.—A long weary march, and we did not get in till much after dark.

On the road we stopped and had some refreshment at a tea-house by the roadside. The tea-houses on this road are innumerable, it being a great trade route; they are open to the streets, and have forms and tables arranged in rows, and various sorts of eatables are supplied at very moderate rates to suit the purses of the patrons, who are mostly coolies in the tea trade. For four cash[1] one gets a little dry tea in a cup, and hot water *ad lib.* Lodinshoma, a large town, boasts of an iron chain bridge in such a state that it is positively dangerous.

27th February; 34 miles, Kholon Fi.—A long

[1] 400 cash = 1 rupee.

march, and when darkness set in, I found myself on a hill-side. However, from a house close by a bundle of canes of a sort that burnt like a torch was procured, and by its aid the halting-place was reached at 9.30 P.M.

20th February; 33 miles.—Over a pass, the last bit of which was on snow, and then into a valley with hill-sides covered with cultivation. The way the Chinese manage to cultivate a mountainous country is marvellous; apparently inaccessible spots boast a little patch growing beans or something of a similar nature, and even the tops of boulders are sometimes covered with soil and crops.

29th February, Chin Chi Sha.—Before marching in the morning we got rid of the palkis and their bearers, and hired ponies instead. Right glad we were to see the last of them—a more lazy insolent lot it has never been my fortune to meet. Being able to go along, keeping up with the caravan, and getting in before dark, was very different from finding oneself stranded when darkness came on, 7 or 8 miles from the halting-place, as had invariably happened when we had travelled by palanquin.

1st March; 27 miles, Khoni Fu.—Crossed our last pass—thank goodness it was the last. Since leaving Leh the number crossed was simply innumerable, but now it was down hill all the way to Shanghai. No more snow, and very little cold to be expected.

2nd March, Chin Thin Tan.—A nice easy march down a valley containing a stream, which was crossed once by a ferry. The climate had completely changed, being much warmer; and clumps of bamboos surrounding the villages gave to the country an almost tropical appearance. There are coal mines somewhere about, as we met numbers of men carrying baskets of coal on their backs. The people, though a little too inquisitive to be pleasant, were still civil, contrasting very favourably with their fellow-countrymen in Kuchar, Aksu, and the other towns of Eastern Turkistan; but as yet we had not been in anything worthy of being called a town, and my experience has always been that the Chinese in villages and the Chinese in towns are two very different races of people. On the road a good many tea bushes were seen—old, unkept, and untrimmed stumps that no Indian tea-planter would ever allow to cumber his ground.

3rd March; 32 miles, Ya Chu or Yatu.—Over a slight ridge, and then down into a country densely populated, as is all the country around. The Chinese are thoroughly alive to the value of manure as a fertiliser. As we left the last place a number of boys followed our ponies with baskets in order to pick up what fell. They have other methods also of enriching the soil. If the people of India would take a lesson from them, not copying all their methods, but only the most commendable of them, it would improve the condition of the country immensely. The indifference with which they regard heaps of excellent fertiliser lying at their doors while their fields are starving for want of it, distresses any one with their welfare at heart. The Chinese are better cultivators than the Hindustanis. Ya Chu is a fairly large town. When we got in, a messenger arrived from the yamen asking permission to copy our passport, which he was allowed to do; and I then proceeded to arrange for a raft to Kiating. A sort of contractor came up and demanded ninety rupees for the job; I offered him ten rupees, which he took with joy. I must have ridiculously overpaid him.

4th March.—Marching over; nothing to do but sit still on a raft and float down. These rafts are wonderful craft; they are made of one layer of bamboos, lashed together with strips of bamboo bark. As the water washes freely over and through them, the baggage has to be elevated on pedestals to keep it dry. They are wonderfully buoyant, carrying heavy loads, and shoot rapids in an extraordinary manner. Knocking against rocks or the bottom does them absolutely no harm whatever; their elasticity saves them. The country on each side of the river was hilly and densely populated, and, though one could hardly say why, it had a thoroughly Chinese appearance. The celestials seem to have a gift of stamping the marks of their presence on the very face of nature. The principal crops appeared to be mustard and rice.

At night we tied up by the bank and slept in a Chinese inn.

5th March.—We had hoped to reach Kiating,

but failed to do so, and spent a cold, miserable, drizzling wet day sitting on the raft, tucking up our feet to keep them dry as we rushed through the rapids, and putting them down again as we got into still water. The river was crowded with duck, but, alas! we had not a single cartridge left.

We passed a great number of boats and rafts being towed up the river; instead of ropes strips of bamboo bark fastened together are used—an excellent material, being light and strong. In the shops and bazaars on the river-bank the amount of sweets and small cakes displayed was very noticeable; many of them were excellent and absurdly cheap. The Chinese undoubtedly bring more intelligence to bear on their cooking arrangements than the natives of India do, the latter having practically no variety at all, though without in any way infringing on caste rules many appetising dishes might be made; but no, "It is not custom," is a native's invariable reply when anything of the nature of change is suggested. In spite of their kickshaws, however, the Chinese can't breed people like the fighting races of Northern India, who man for man would be hard to beat in any company, the reason probably being that in one case the staple article of food is rice and in the other wheat. I was much struck with the amount of rice the boatmen managed to put away, but they could not hold a candle to the palki-bearers, who seemed to stop for a little light refreshment at every tea-house they came to.

Coffin-making seems a very flourishing industry in China. As we floated down the river numbers of coffins were to be seen piled up outside the places where they were made.

6th March, Kiating.—Shortly after midday, Kiating, a large walled town, picturesquely situated on the left bank of the river, was reached. It is a place of considerable importance, doing a large trade in silk, etc.

Directly we got in, I proceeded to arrange for a boat to take us to Chung King, and after some bargaining got a fair-sized one for 8 taels. The owner wanted half in advance, but after weighing a number of bits of silver, the nearest I could get to it was 2½ taels, so the remainder had to be given to him in cash (400 cash = 1 rupee), of which it took 2200 to make up the amount. The want of a coinage in China is a great nuisance when travelling; as it is often impossible to make up the exact weight required in the lumps of silver used, and the difference having to be made up in cash, a large quantity of them has to be carried, a matter of little moment with water carriage, but a serious matter with coolie or pony transport,—a whole pony-load of them only represents a small sum. In the evening, just after we had gone to bed, we were surprised by hearing our boat hailed from the bank in English; the unexpected visitor turned out to be Mr. Rarey, of the China Inland Mission, who had been three years in this out-of-the-way place. He told us that in two days we should reach Sui Fu, where there were several missionaries.

8th March.—We reached Sui Fu just before dark, and started at once to call on Mr. and Mrs. Faers of the mission, whom we found in a native house close to the north gate. Their house, with a few European things about, appeared quite comfortable, but living in the midst of a Chinese town cannot be pleasant. Both of them, as is the usual custom in the mission, were dressed in Chinese clothes.

A crowd had followed us through the streets and remained outside, screaming and hooting while we were inside. Suddenly the noise became much louder, and we rushed out to see what had happened, and found the excitement was all owing to my spaniel having gone out, creating a panic amongst the mob, who were terrified at the sight of the foreign dog, while he was no less terrified at the hubbub.

In the East a difficulty in understanding European philanthropy is often met with, but there are no people to whom it is so incomprehensible as the Chinese. For two hundred years missionaries have been established here, and yet Mr. and Mrs. Faers were lately in considerable danger owing to a report having been spread that they had stolen a child and eaten it, the child in question having simply strayed; fortunately it was found just in time to prevent anything serious occurring. As the continual outbreaks against missionaries in places in which they have been long established show, attempting to live these ideas down and gain the confidence of the people seems a hopeless task. The people at large will much more readily believe that the missionaries come for the purpose of obtaining the flesh of Chinese children to eat or some mysterious medicine to be obtained from their brains, than that they came for purposes dictated by philanthropy. Mr. Faers was kind enough to see us down to our boat, and it was very fortunate he did so, as the mob were rather obstreperous, and followed calling out impertinences of different sorts. Mr. Faers, by turning round and speaking to them in their own language, managed to keep them within bounds. What made the chances of a row greater than they would usually be was that the town was full of military students up for one of the periodical examinations: these military students are for the most part composed of the lowest class of the people, coolies, etc.; the principal part of the examination consists of shooting five arrows at a mark, and riding a horse along a trench, letting go the reins and swinging the arms about. Bribery does not play such an important part in the military examinations as it does in the civil, owing to the greater poverty of the candidates and the much smaller prizes to be obtained. Mr. Faers told me of a case he knew of, in which in a civil examination a candidate had given a bribe of 1000 taels. We passed a man in the street who was shouting out filthy and disgusting language, being, we were informed, paid to do so. Verily the Chinese are a strange people.

9th March.—Off down the river again with the earliest streaks of daylight. Just below Sui Fu the main stream of the Yang-tse-Kiang, crowded with junks coming up with sails of matting spread, was reached. On the bank a number of heads that had belonged to criminals of the petty river pirate order were exhibited; the exhibition of criminals' heads is a regular Chinese custom, and no doubt has a deterrent effect.

Of all people in the world there is none that I have seen that have such a general sickly appearance as the Chinese. Looking at a crowd of them, one hardly sees a single healthy-looking face, probably owing to the vicious lives they lead, as the climate is healthy enough. On the sea-coast, amongst the boating population, it is not so noticeable; a man who is out in a boat all day is not as likely to ruin his constitution or to be naturally as depraved as the denizens of inland cities. I should hesitate to commit myself to the statement that it is because the coast people smoke Indian opium and the inland people native-grown; as the amount of Indian opium imported is so small in comparison to the amount grown, that its effects on the people cannot be noticeable one way or the other.

10th March.—As soon as it got dark we tied up by the bank for the night. In the bazaar close by pigs', cats' and dogs' flesh was exhibited for sale; the two latter evidently are held in small estimation compared with the former, as, though pork cost from

80 to 120 cash a jing, dog's flesh only cost 40, and cat's 25.

11th, 12th, and 13th March.—We were delayed by head winds, and continually had to tie up by the bank until the wind moderated, so we did not reach Chung King till the 13th. Chung King is a large town of about two hundred thousand inhabitants, situated at the junction of two rivers. A considerable trade in white wax, silk, etc., is done, and if steamers only ran up as far, being as it is the entrepôt for trade with the enormous province of Szechuen, it would develop into a second Shanghai. As soon as we got in we started off to call on Mr. Fulford, the British Consul. The road lay through the city, in which there are several good shops. It was very evident that we had got into a country where the people had a certain knowledge of Europeans, as the prices asked were much higher than were asked farther back in places where Europeans were unknown. The British Consulate is a native building inside the town, and in no way suitable. For one thing it is not right that a European gentleman should be expected to live in an evil-smelling insanitary Chinese city; but I believe that in order that he may maintain his influence with the native officials, it is considered advisable that he should do so; and, secondly, it is not dignified that the representative of a great power should be so meanly lodged. We were unfortunate in finding Mr. Fulford from home, and as it was uncertain when he would return, we went back

A GORGE ON THE YANG-TSE-KIANG.

to our boat much disappointed. In the evening we received a note from him, asking us to be his guests during our stay. Unfortunately it was too late to avail ourselves of his kind offer then as the city gates were just closing, but we promised to be with him in the morning.

Next day we went to see him. It was a great treat,—meeting a fellow-countryman and feeling oneself in touch once more with civilisation; the looking over old papers, and reading up nearly a year's news, was very interesting. An arrangement was also made during the day with a man for a boat to Ichang. In return for eighteen taels we were to be delivered there in eight days or less, and one tael was to be deducted from the amount for each day over eight. The whole arrangement was written out and signed.

In the afternoon we went to call on Mr. Hobson and Mr. Lovett, of the Imperial Customs Service; their quarters are infinitely superior to the Consulate. Here, as at Sui Fu, the place was full of military students, who were to be seen practising archery in every available spot. I fancy the Chinese Government are fully alive to the fact that bows and arrows are obsolete, but they don't put enough faith in the students to let them handle better weapons.

The severity of the civil examinations (which is slightly tempered with bribery) may be judged from the fact that after local examinations had been held all over the province, fifteen thousand successful candidates appeared at Chentu, the capital, for further examination, and from amongst those a very small number would be allowed to go to Pekin for the final.

Though Chung King is nominally an open port, steamers are not allowed to run to it, the reason alleged by the Chinese being that opposition would occasion disturbances amongst the boating population who at present do the carrying work. This at first sight may appear an excellent argument, but experience has shown that when a port is thrown open to steam traffic, the trade increases so enormously that the work for the boats and junks in no way diminishes; in fact the boating population benefits as much as anybody else. For instance, between Hankau and Shanghai, where nine-tenths of the traffic is carried on steamers, there are more junks on the river than before Hankau was an open port. Whether steamers could run up to Chung King or not is a question on which I cannot feel myself justified in giving a decided opinion, but I certainly saw no steamer in China that could do so,—specially constructed ones might possibly be able to.

Outside the city for miles the country is one large graveyard. On certain occasions the people burn immense quantities of papers to the manes of their ancestors, a regular place being established for the purpose. The size to which the graveyards extend often becomes a serious question, as the only occasion on which the levelling of them is held to be justifiable is on the occurrence of a change of dynasty.

15th March.—After staying at Mr. Fulford's for the night we went aboard our boat at daylight expecting to start at once, but unfortunately some of the boatmen had not arrived, so we were kept waiting a couple of hours before we got off.

Just below Chung King, owing to the junction of the tributary coming from Chentu, the river is half as big again as above it. Though the boat was much larger than the one we had come in, we were rather more than less crowded owing to the increased number of rowers, and there was just lying-down accommodation for all hands and nothing more. The boatmen rowed with long sweeps, standing up, and kept up a not unmusical sort of refrain all the time; they seemed a cheerful lot.

Many large junks were met coming up the river with sails set and men on shore towing as well. We were never tired of admiring the animated scene the river presented, backed as it was by a beautiful fertile country. When we landed anywhere the people would follow us about making insolent remarks, but on turning round suddenly it was most amusing to see the way they took to their heels.

17th March, Wanchu.—We managed to leave a good many miles behind us, as starting shortly after midnight we kept going steadily until 8 P.M. A gentle breeze astern was all the wind we had, whereas most days we had had a strong breeze against us, more particularly in the afternoon. On the way we passed the village of Szi Po Chai, where there is a most remarkably picturesque rock with perpendicular sides. Against one side there is a seven-storied pagoda and on the top there are some buildings.

Wanchu is a large place on the river bank; as is common at many places, grass huts are erected below the summer level of the river to serve as tea-houses for the boating population.

18th March.—It rained hard, and soon after starting we had to tie up by the bank quite unable to make any way against the strong head wind that was blowing. It was rather miserable work sitting there hour after hour, but there was no remedy. At last the wind moderated, and we started again and just managed to reach the town of Yi Young Shung as darkness set in.

19th March.—Well into the celebrated Yangtse gorges, where the hills are much higher and more barren than those higher up; looking either ahead or astern, along stretches of the river, it seemed as if there was no outlet, and that we were in a long narrow lake.

Along the face of the cliffs runs a path cut out of the solid rock in many places, all the work of a private individual. Such deeds are thoroughly in accordance with Eastern ideas, the country being largely dependent on the philanthropy or vanity of private individuals for works which in the west would be undertaken by the State. Towards the lower end there are some rather nasty rapids. Possibly with more water in the river they might be passable for steamers, but as we saw them they certainly were not.

On the 22nd we emerged from the gorges, and rounding a bend in the river, H.M.S. *Esk*, a Chinese revenue cruiser, and the s.s. *Y Ling* came in sight, anchored off the town of Ichang, the furthermost from the sea of all the open ports. We went straight alongside the *Y Ling*, but were much disappointed to find that she was full up and could not take us, a mandarin with the usual following of rag-tag and bob-tail having monopolised the passenger accommodation, so we had to make up our minds to wait for the next steamer, whose arrival was very uncertain owing to the low state of the river. We then went to call on Mr. Everard, the British Consul, who lives quite near to the river. Close by, a remembrance of the disturbances that had occurred a few months previously was to be seen in the blackened walls of the mission buildings burnt down by the rioters. The Chinese are a people of indomitable valour when several thousand of them are pitted against a few unarmed missionaries, but their valour is of a kind that evaporates wonderfully quickly in front of a few rifles in the hands of determined men. After they had destroyed the mission station, in a fit of elation they rushed to the Custom-house, but there a surprise party in the shape of eight Europeans with rifles awaited them—a *dénouement* as disagreeable as it was unexpected; so the valorous rabble quietly melted away.

In the evening we heard that the mandarin who was going in the *Y Ling* had changed his mind about going, so we should be able to go in her after all, and we took our things on board at once, rejoicing to think that we had done with uncivilised modes of travel; steamboat and rail were to take the place of caravan and native boats, and the commissariat was no longer to be a daily source of anxiety.

Before daylight we were under weigh, and on going on deck found ourselves steaming through a country of quite a different character from what it is above Ichang. The hills had given place to a flat alluvial country, and the river had widened out tremendously. Opposite Sha Szi, a large town on the banks, we stopped and anchored, in order to take off and discharge passengers; as it is not a treaty port, the loading and discharging of cargo is forbidden.

Next day we passed Sandy Island, where a sandbank stretches right across the river. As it is always shifting, and there is very little water on it, it is a continual source of anxiety to captains of steamers. We just managed to get over it and nothing more. All this part of the river is pretty ticklish navigation; ships continually stick and are often on a sandbank for some days, and eventually get off either by the rising of the water or by taking the cargo out and hauling off. Numbers of rafts were passed floating down; they are of immense size, and have huts built on them in which regular communities live.

A Norwegian missionary came on board at a small town *en route;* he seemed very devoted to his work, but had the usual story to tell of not much success so far, but great hopes.

On 26th March we reached Hankau, the great tea-mart of China. Finding that the s.s. *Kiang Yu* was to start that evening for Shanghai, we got our things on board at once. She is a magnificent specimen of a river steamer.

After getting our things on board, we went to have a look round the settlement. Along the river's edge there is a bund (embankment), much used as a promenade. Behind it are the merchants' and other residents' houses and offices, and though not quite so fine, they distinctly resemble the Chowringhee houses in Calcutta. They are certainly more comfortable than the ordinary up-country Indian bungalows; but the absence of gardens and the way the houses are crowded together constitute great drawbacks to an Anglo-Indian eye.

Hankau boasts a small racecourse, seven furlongs round. The only racing in China is pony-racing, so the smallness of the course cannot be considered much of a disadvantage. I saw some of the ponies being walked on the course. So far as I could see, they were all what are known in Central Asia as Kalmacks, a breed that comes from about Mongolia; heavy-headed, coarse animals, with thick tails, up to weight and good baggage animals, but not racers. Indian country-bred ponies could gallop away from the best of them. However, the sport is just as good, whether as a class the horses are slow or fast, provided that none from another class are introduced.

In the evening we dined with Mr. Moorhead, the popular Commissioner of Customs, and had the pleasure of meeting several of the residents. It was a pleasant evening, cut short by our having to be on board the steamer by 10 P.M.

27th March.—Steaming down the Yangtse against a head wind, rain falling all day. About 2 P.M. we arrived at the open port of Kiu-Kiang, celebrated as being the place where most of the china for the Emperor is made. It is distinguishable from ordinary china by the dragon on it being five-toed. Great quantities are rejected for some microscopic or imaginary fault, and all rejected articles are condemned to be broken, but as a matter of fact are generally sold.

Wusue, where two inoffensive unarmed Englishmen had lately been done to death by the mob, was also passed—a mob who, if they had been confronted by a dozen armed men either before, after, or during the time they were actually killing these men, would have cringed and protested their good intentions.

A very conspicuous island, called the Little Orphan, is passed farther down the river. The legend is that a father and mother and two children were coming up stream in a boat, when a squall struck them and they were capsized; the parents were drowned, but a turtle took the children on his back; one, however, was washed off, and formed the Little Orphan, the other was washed off farther up and formed the Big Orphan, and the turtle swimming on at last grounded and formed a third island.

The large city of Nankin, celebrated for the part it played in the Taeping rebellion, was passed on the 28th. It was held for a long time by the rebels against the Imperialists, who built works on the other side of the river, and exchanged shots, that never did any one any harm, with the besieged. The Imperialists got a celebrated river pirate, much dreaded by the Government, to help them, but all he did was to levy a duty on cargoes of rice going to the beleaguered city.

Nowadays the river front is protected by Krupp guns, that, in case of war, it would be as well to take before ships passed in front, as the river is rather narrow at that part.

Some idea of the magnitude of Chinese works may be judged from the fact that the walls of Nankin are twenty-one miles round. Of course the city only occupies a small part of the space thus enclosed. The Chinese certainly spend an enormous amount on defensive works. All over the kingdom it is the same. Every city has a wall round it, though in many cases, owing to hills commanding the town, the walls are of no value whatever. The Great Wall, an attempt to make the whole country into one great fort, gives a good clue to Chinese ideas as regards military matters. They don't like the idea of fighting in the open. At the slightest disturbance they rush into their forts and shut the doors.

On the 29th, at 11 A.M., we reached the mouth of the Wangpo river, at which there are some Chinese forts armed with modern guns. Their value, however, is much diminished by their being entrenched to such an extent that they have practically no lateral range whatever.

Shanghai is thirteen miles from the mouth of the river. All the way up ships of all nations were to be met *en route* to the ocean, while off the town a dozen or so of gunboats were anchored, bearing about them that quiet air of subdued potentiality that seems so inherent in warships. Animation was given to the scene by the innumerable brightly-coloured sampans flitting hither and thither on shore. The settlement itself, including a brewery, cotton mills, water-work, and the quays, gave evidence of European skill and enterprise.

At the wharf a crowd of Chinese with jinrikshaws and barrows was assembled to meet us, and getting through them was rather a business. Shanghai is called, and deservedly so, "the model settlement," but a sweeping reform would be the abolition of some of the jinrikshaws. It is impossible to walk in any comfort along the streets owing to the way one is pestered by their owners, otherwise the most captious critic would find little to cavil at in Shanghai. With its well-laid-out clean streets, electric light, etc., it has little to learn from other places, though it is by no means the only place in the east laying claim to the title of "the model settlement."

In the police they have sixty Sikhs who do excellent work. They were delighted to have a talk with any one from the Punjab, and we conversed about the Dewali at Amritsar and other matters of much interest to those hailing from the "land of the five rivers." They seemed very contented with their lot, and had a supreme contempt for the Chinese, nor does one require to be long in Shanghai to see the dread with which they are regarded by the Celestials.

From Shanghai we went in the Messageries Maritimes steamer *Natal* to Hongkong, thence in the s.s. *Japan viâ* Singapore and Penang, both "model settlements" that, strange to say, though almost smothered in vegetation, can grow no vegetables, to Calcutta. From here we went direct to Simla, which we reached after an absence of twelve and a half months.

The caravan drivers went straight on in the train to Rawal Pindi, whence their homes in Ladakh could be reached in a month. They had done good service. Without their assistance the trip could never have been brought to a successful termination. When tired and hungry they never hesitated to start after ponies that had strayed, and often were out after them all night. The way—day after day for months—they had marched, exposed to all sorts of weather and hardships, exemplified well the lasting power of the oriental when well fed. During the greater part of the journey they had had plenty of meat, which had rendered the amount of work they had done possible.

Parting with them was a painful business, and I shall ever think kindly of the men to whom I owe so much.

CHAPTER XVI

RELIGION, COUNTRY, PEOPLE, ETC.

In the North-West Provinces of India, about 2500 years ago, Siddharta Gautama, surnamed Buddha, or "the enlightened one," originated the religion called after him. Its rapid success in obtaining converts was probably largely due to a reactionary feeling against the oppressive distinctions of caste imposed by the Brahmins; but there appears to have been little, if any, ill-feeling between the followers of Gautama and the adherents of the more ancient Hinduism. We have the evidence of the two Chinese pilgrims, Fa Hien, who visited India in the fourth century, and Hwen Tsang, who visited it in the seventh, that the two religions lived amicably side by side. The history of both shows a striking absence of anything of the nature of religious persecution or intolerance, a point in which they compare most favourably with the more aggressive Mohammedanism. Buddhism is a religion of a decidedly mild and negative character. Existence it holds to be misery, and contemplation a virtue,—doctrines it is impossible to conceive as being an incentive to great or good actions; but there is nothing in such ideas incompatible with friendship towards the adherents of other creeds.

The number of people who can be classed as Buddhists has been very much exaggerated, some writers going the length of estimating it at a third of the human race, their numbers being arrived at by including the whole of the Chinese race—a great mistake; the mass of the Chinese people are Taoists and Confucianists in theory, while in practice veneration of ancestors is the form their religion takes. If statistical reports of a reliable nature could ever be obtained of the people professing the different religions in China, most people would be astonished at the number of Mussulmans and the few Buddhists the Empire contains.

That even the Tibetans should be classed as Buddhists appears to me to be a question quite open to discussion; when first the religion was introduced into the country from India, it came strongly impregnated with Hinduism, as is testified by the idols to be seen on Mānés, and in houses, the great majority of which are taken from the Hindu Pantheon. On its arrival in Tibet it was largely influenced by Shamanism, and yet still more modified by the introduction of Lamaism. From these various sources and influences the modern religion of Tibet has sprung—a religion that does not appear to be correctly described as Buddhism. Travelling through the country one sees little that can be connected with

Gautama or his doctrines, certainly not more than can be connected with Hinduism. Caste is absent, but that can easily be accounted for by the fact that the Brahman race never obtained a foothold in the country, and the Lamas being nominally celibate, cannot arrogate to themselves any peculiar racial superiority. But even caste, though intimately bound up with the Hindu religion, is not an integral part of it, but merely a social institution.

Writers differ very much as to the actual date at which Buddhism crossed the Himalayas; but its having come in such a Hinduised form points to its introduction having been comparatively recent, as the probable ending of the religion in India was that it became so impregnated with Brahmanism as not to be distinguishable from it, and it must have been in a transition state when it obtained a foothold in Tibet. In no country is religion so much *en évidence;* every man has a praying-wheel in his hand which he continually turns, even when on horseback; piles of stones engraved with mystical sentences are met with; flags bearing the same mystical sentences flutter in the wind; and in the very hills and rocks they are inscribed. But all this outward show means nothing but a gross superstition; in no way do the people regard their religion as being a rule of life inculcating virtue and morality; all they think is that, by observing certain rules, benefit—but they know not what benefit—is obtained, and by neglecting them, calamities—but they know not what calamities—would ensue.

The head of the Tibetan government, both in things spiritual and in things temporal, is the Talai Lama; but in order that he may the better attend to heavenly matters, and have ample time for undisturbed contemplation and meditation, he is assisted by a governor to whom a great part of his power is delegated. This governor may be regarded as the most powerful man in the country. He again is assisted by a Chasag, or secretary, also a man of great weight in the state, as all communications for the governor go through him, and he decides many matters without reference to his superiors. Unfortunately Talai Lamas, who are supposed to come of age at eighteen, almost invariably die before attaining their majority; or, to express it more correctly according to Tibetan ideas, disgusted with the sins of the world, they retire to the mansions of joy, a retirement that almost invariably takes place before they reach the age appointed for taking over the seal of office. That the retirement is due to the sins of the world few people will be inclined to doubt; but a *post mortem* would probably show that it was hardly voluntary, and without the evidence of a *post mortem* we may safely assume, from the prevalence of poisoning in the country, that that is the means of their death, and as the power remains with the Gyalpos (literally kings) or regents, the motive is not far to seek.

After death the Talai Lama once more becomes incarnate in a child, and the priests go to look for him. Assisted by divine inspiration they fix on some child who, on reaching four years of age, is tested by being called upon to identify property belonging to the deceased; he is almost invariably successful, and is then removed to the monastery of Potala, where he spends the remainder of his life. Should he by any chance be unsuccessful, the monks recommence their search; and when the matter is finally settled, intimation is sent to the Emperor of China, not for confirmation, but simply for information. Two interpretations of the word Talai are given, some identifying it with the Mongolian word for *ocean*,[1] and others deriving it from the Chinese, the root being the word *Ta*, great. In Tibet the commonest word used for the Talai Lama is Deva Zhung, or "happiness centre"; it is applied both to him personally and to the central government at Lhasa.

The Talai Lama, the Tesho Lama or Grand Lama, and the Gyalpos, all belong to the reformed monks of the Ge-luks-pa (virtuous ones) or yellow order, though the name "yellow order," usually applied by Europeans to the sect founded by the great reformer Tsong Kharpa, in the fourteenth century, is apt to be misleading, as ordinarily they dress in the same dingy red garments as the unreformed monks, their caps only being yellow. Next to the governor comes the Council of Kahlons, or ministers. Up till quite recently there were only four of them, but in accordance

[1] The meaning of the word "Dalai" (Talai) is simply *Ocean*; this term having been adopted, probably, to convey the idea of vastness and grandeur (W. F. Mayers in *Journal of the Royal Asiatic Society*, N. S. iv. 304. 1869).

with the ever-increasing power of the Church a fifth member, chosen from the priesthood, has been added, nominally to look after the interests of the Church. Subordinate to the Kahlons are sixteen officials, of whom four are charged with civil administration, four with military matters, four with justice, and four with finance. In addition to these officials, in every district there are administrative officers who are entrusted with powers of jurisdiction within the limits of their districts.

However well this constitution may look upon paper, in reality the whole country is in the hands of an overweening priesthood; who to the power granted them by law and custom, add the fearful weapon that superstition places in their hands, to grind the people down to a condition that certainly, as regards those living round the monasteries in church lands, is little better than slavery, and as regards the rest, is far from the state of freedom under which nations develop and civilisation advances.

The population of Tibet proper, in the country under the rule of the Deva Zhung, may be estimated at 4,000,000; but Chinese Tibet, together with Kham, which is really governed by its own chiefs, may be taken as holding another 4,000,000, thus giving a total of 8,000,000 Tibetans, of whom probably half a million are monks. Looking at the enormous stretch of country over which these 8,000,000 are distributed, it is apparent that the country is extremely sparsely populated. There are several reasons for this:—primarily the custom of polyandry, which, though not universally, is still largely practised; secondly, the large number of monks, who, though probably only nominally celibate, are forbidden to marry; and thirdly, although the country in certain parts, more particularly towards the east, could support a slightly larger population than it does at present, the greater part is only capable of supporting wild yak and antelope. Polyandry, we may safely assume, was originally introduced on economic grounds by some far-seeing statesman, who realised that in a country where so little land was capable of being brought under cultivation, a large increase in the population must either lead to great poverty or emigration, and emigration is rendered out of the question by the fact that Tibetans are quite incapable of living out of their own country,—moved to a more genial climate they quickly sicken. The practical value of polyandry is plainly demonstrated when we regard Ladakh and Baltistan, two countries inhabited by a similar Mongolian race of people, differing only in religion. In Baltistan they are Mohammedans, following the precepts of that religion as regards their marriage customs, the result being over-population and extreme poverty; while, in Ladakh, Buddhism and plurality of husbands lead to comparative plenty.

The whole of Central and Northern Tibet, and almost the whole of Western Tibet, is called the Chang; it consists of a high table-land, with hills mostly of a rounded character, with broad open valleys between, but here and there sharply-defined massy ranges are met with. The mountains have a general east and west tendency, but no defined watershed exists, and all the rivers terminate in salt lakes, which appear to be gradually drying up, as unmistakable signs that at one time they occupied much more extended areas than they do at present, are to be seen. The whole of the Chang itself, however, forms a most distinct watershed: the rivers rising on the east find their way to Burma and China, while those rising on the south and west, penetrating the barrier of the Himalayas, emerge on the plains of India.

An idea of the general configuration of the country may be gathered from the fact that from the end of June until the middle of November the average altitude of our camps was over 16,000 feet, the lowest being 14,621 feet, and the highest 18,315 feet, while the highest pass crossed was 18,760 feet. All the enormous stretch of country crossed in that time contained not a single tree, and only two species of shrub, and these rarely exceeded 6 inches in height; flowering plants and grasses however were found, and Dr. Thorold collected 115 species, one of which was found at an altitude of 19,000 feet, probably the greatest height at which any flowering plant has been collected. Great stretches of this Chang afford excellent grazing in summer, but are too far from suitable winter quarters to be made use of by the nomads, so they are left to the wild yak, antelope, and gazelle, which are never disturbed, except by some wandering bands of Chukpas (brigands) who find these wastes an excellent asylum whence to swoop down on the tents of the nomads living on the border, or to retire to when pursued.

The nomads, on whom these brigands prey, are a purely pastoral people, living almost entirely on the produce of their flocks and herds—vegetables and fruits they can never taste—and "tsampa," a kind of barley flour, the only starchy food their tents ever boast, which is regarded as a luxury to be partaken of sparingly. Their tents are of rough blackish sacking, made of yak and goats' hair, and with a slit in the top through which the smoke escapes; in winter a wall of cow-dung is built on the west side as a protection from the prevailing wind, while stacks of it stored as fuel are to be seen outside. The higher officials have tents made of cotton, and ornamented with mysterious designs.

Descending from the Chang, after passing through the belt of country occupied by the nomads, at an altitude of about 13,500 feet, cultivation, consisting principally of barley, is met with, accompanied, as cultivation always is, by houses and a settled people. The country here is of quite a different character. The rounded bare hills give place to steep well-wooded mountains, the broad open valleys are replaced by narrow deep gorges, down which the waters from the melting snows flow, and end, not like the rivers of the Chang, after a few miles of sluggish course in a dead salt lake, but ever being reinforced, and ever increasing in volume and power, they develop into the mighty Yang-tse-Kiang, and Mekong, and having crossed China and Indo-China, end their courses in the sea.

The character of all the Tibetans settled and nomadic is much the same,—cowardly, faithless, and immoral; to those they are afraid of they are servile, to those they are not afraid of, insolent; and the Lamas, in whose hands they are mere slaves, rule them with a rod of iron, by working on their superstitious fears. In Eastern Tibet their faithlessness and unreliability have been shown by the way that on the slightest sign of an anti-foreign disturbance they have deserted the French missionaries, to whom they owed so much, and to whose religion they had become converts. Their physique is distinctly good, and they appear to be able to stand almost any amount of cold and hunger. Less industrious and skilful than the Chinese, they are still an active lively people, and at first one is inclined to regard them as simple, light-hearted, and lovable; but subsequent experiences only demonstrate the inadvisability of allowing oneself to be led away by first impressions. There is little to like in them, and they are only one degree less cunning than their neighbours the Chinese.

The dress of the common people consists of a long sheepskin robe, very dirty, and very greasy; this is hitched up by a waist-belt during the day in such a manner that, while the upper part is very full, the lower part hangs down to the knees like a kilt. At night they take off the belt and allow the robe to come down to the feet; it thus serves the double purpose of clothes by day and bedding by night. In warm weather, or what they consider warm weather, the right arm is bare, being thrust out of the coat; in the waist, stuck diagonally across the front of the body, a straight sword in a scabbard, ornamented with silver incrustations and torquoises, is carried; a matchlock with a two-pronged rest is generally slung across the shoulders; and in their hands a long spear is often to be seen. On their feet they have stockings of brightly coloured woollen cloth, soled with yak's hide, and coming up to the knee, where they are fastened by garters. The love of jewellery and ornaments is a very marked trait in their character, and the amount of the precious metals used up in this way in the country must be very great indeed. The richer people affect red woollen clothes, similar to those worn by the monks, and various coloured silks.

As the Chinese in the country, not being allowed by the Tibetans to bring women with them across the bridge at Nagchuka, take unto themselves wives of the country, there must be a certain mixture of races, particularly on the main road to Lhasa, where there are a few Chinese stationed at each of the rest-houses; but the children seem to grow up thoroughly Tibetan; and passing through the country one does not see any people that strike one as being half-breeds, though, on inquiry, people that are the result of these mixed marriages are pointed out.

Amongst all classes—officials, Lamas, peasants, and nomads—a taste for trading is strongly developed, and all are ever ready to seize an opportunity for making money. The higher officials more particularly devote themselves to commerce, as the emoluments appertaining to their offices are exceedingly small, but the position gives them ample opportunities to trade with advantage; and these opportunities none fail to avail themselves of. The Lamas utilise portions of the great wealth their monasteries contain for trading purposes, the peasants nearly all devote a certain amount of attention to commerce, and the nomads are ever ready to dispose of wool and hides. Formerly the trade with Ta chen Lu was entirely in the hands of the Chinese, but the Tibetans have shown their commercial capabilities by almost completely ousting the Celestials, and now go there themselves to make purchases. As regards prospects of trade with India, should the country ever be open to commerce, of all articles in which we can hope to do a profitable trade tea easily ranks first; at one time it was a government monopoly, and even now I believe it is compulsorily sold to the people in some parts, the pressure being put on by members of the government engaged in the trade. The population of Tibet, that is to say of Tibet proper, has been estimated at four millions. If they drank as much tea per head as is drunk in England, viz. 5 lbs., the annual consumption would be twenty million pounds; and even taking the consumption per head at the low figure of 3 lbs., that would give a total of twelve million pounds, but so far as a traveller can tell simply passing through the country, a very much larger amount per head is consumed than in England. Mixed with butter and salt, and forming to European tastes a most unpalatable-looking mixture, it is always in evidence both in the nomads' tents and the peasants' houses. During all discussions, whether it is a meeting of Kahlons to settle affairs of state or some mendicants crouching over a fire, each man has a cup in front of him, which is continually being replenished, and a stranger entering a tent or a house most probably finds the inhabitants drinking it. From Lhasa to Ta chen Lu the string of yaks, mules, and ponies laden with brick tea to meet this enormous demand is continuous. These bricks appear to be made from the prunings of neglected bushes of extreme age, and are quite the worst tea I have ever seen, worse even than the tea exported from Leh into Chinese Turkistan, which at one time I thought was the worst in the world,—but at that time I was not fully acquainted with the Chinaman's capabilities for producing bad tea, and probably would not have recognised the vegetable matter imported into Tibet as being tea, but would have hesitated before deciding as to whether it was compressed fodder or some form of portable fuel. Ordinarily, it is packed in bamboo matting, but some of the finer qualities, most of which are finer only by comparison, and are imported for the use of the higher dignitaries, are also packed in hide. That Tibet is much more accessible from the gardens of India than from the tea-growing districts of China is a plain geographical fact, and we can only hope that some day the market may be thrown open to our Darjiling planters; but to meet the popular taste they would have to make brick tea. Amongst a nomadic people, and a large proportion of the population of Tibet is more or less nomadic, it is more popular than loose tea, as it carries better and weathers less. The fine classes of tea would probably not be fully appreciated in Tibet, as the delicate aroma would materially suffer when churned up with butter and salt.

Besides tea, other articles that would find a market are sugar, tobacco, rice, knives, crockery, tinted spectacles, red and yellow broadcloth, brass buttons, brightly-stamped cotton cloth, and coral.

Amongst the articles that Tibet can export, wool takes the foremost place; the capabilities of the country as regards the amount that could be supplied are practically unlimited. A large proportion of the population is essentially pastoral, and in places it would be possible to travel for weeks together and have sheep in sight every day, and nearly all day. Musk also is plentiful and cheap, and readily finds a market in India; and yaks' tails could be supplied in sufficient quantities to meet any probable demand. There is evidently a great accumulation of the precious metals in the country; the women dressed in dirty sheepskins often wear several hundred rupees worth of silver ornaments, while a gold bead here and there is not uncommon; and a man may often be seen drinking tea out of an extremely inferior porcelain cup, with a silver saucer, cover, and spoon. The ratio between gold and silver varies considerably in different localities; Lithang is the place where we found gold cheapest; there its relative value with silver was fourteen to one. In Kashmir the same quality of gold, viz. dust as washed, costs about twenty-two times its weight in silver.

The flora of the Chang is exceedingly poor. Dr. Thorold collected every flowering plant he saw, and yet succeeded in obtaining only 115 species, which, however, were of great interest, being all collected between 15,000 and 19,000 feet. These plants are very characteristic of wind-swept plateaux; only one of them is of a shrubby character, and even it does not rise much above the ground, while the remainder only rise from half an inch to three inches. The grasses, of which twenty-three species were collected, must be extremely nourishing, as, travelling across the plateaux, the enormous herds of yak and antelope to be seen appear quite disproportionate to the amount of grass to support them produced by the country. How these animals live through the arctic cold of the long winter, when the country is covered with snow, hiding the little withered grass that remains at the end of summer, appears a mystery, and can only be accounted for by the amount of fat they lay up when the grass is at its best.

The yak (*Poëphagus grunniens*) is the typical animal of Tibet; herds, and occasionally solitary old bulls, are to be seen all over the Chang. Sometimes as many as a hundred were seen in a day, and for days together some were always in sight. When I mention that the chances are against a sportsman on six months' leave to Chang Chenmo getting a single bull, it will be understood what a happy hunting ground we found ourselves in. They are extremely easy to stalk, their sight not being nearly as acute as that of most wild animals. Their powers of scent are, however, fairly good, and care has to be taken that the wind is in the right direction when approaching them. I have never known one charge, even when wounded and with his assailant in view. Tame yaks are largely used as beasts of burden. They are very surefooted, and carry loads over places where ponies could never go; and their habitat being at great elevations, they are not oppressed by mountain sickness; but they travel very slowly, and soon get footsore. Thus the progeny of Yak bulls and common domestic cows is also largely used.

Tibetan antelope (*Pantholops hodgsonii*) are also very widely distributed over the Chang. Their habitat may be said to commence in the west at the Karakorum Pass, and extends to the Lhasa-Sining road on the east, and probably they are found in occasional patches of suitable country still farther east. On the south they are found on the plateaux north of Sikkim and Kumaun, and towards the north as far as the Tibetan plateau extends. They are most plentiful between 16,000 feet and 18,500, and are very rarely found below 15,000. A peculiarity about them is that in summer the sexes inhabit quite different stretches of country. On the Karakorum, for instance, nothing but does are found on the southern slope, and nothing but males on the northern. They make a form like a hare in the open valleys, and their presence is only detected by the graceful lyre-shaped horns showing above the bare plain. Their flesh is excellent eating, and during our long tramp across the Chang we lived almost entirely on it. Had they not been plentiful and widely distributed, our commissariat would have been a source of much greater anxiety than it was.

The Tibetan gazelle (*Gazella picticaudata*) is even more widely distributed than the antelope, but is nowhere so numerous as antelope are in certain places.

They are handsome little animals, very much resembling the Chinkara of India and Jeran of Turkistan. Shooting them is not nearly such easy work as shooting antelope; in addition to being a much smaller mark to aim at, they are much more wary, and in the most out-of-the-way places fled incontinently directly the caravan was viewed; whereas the antelope continually trotted past, very little, if at all, out of express rifle range. In British territory they are found in the neighbourhood of Hanli and the Tso Morari Lake, in Ladakh; and we found them in Tibet as far east as Asi, on the road between Chiamdo and Garthok. It is probable that they are found as far north as the suitable country exists, that is, plateaux at an elevation of 13,000 to 18,000 feet. In the Gobi Desert their place is taken by *Gazella subgutturosa.*

The Kiang (*Equus hemionus*) belongs to the same class as the ghorkhar of Western India and the zebra of Africa. They are widely distributed over Tibet, where they are very common. In colour they are a sort of chestnut on the upper part of the body, fading into fawn colour and white on the abdomen, and with a dark brown stripe down the back. The mane is thin and erect, and the grace of their appearance is much spoilt by the enormous head and large ears. They are by no means shy, being, on the contrary, very inquisitive, and their ill-timed curiosity often spoils a stalk after nobler game. Sometimes they may be seen wheeling and turning on the Tibetan plains like a troop of cavalry.

The *Ovis ammon* (Tibetan *Nyan*) is the noblest of all Tibetan game, and with the *Ovis poli* of the Pamirs, claims kingship over all the sheep tribe. A full-grown ram stands about 12 hands at the shoulder and its horns measure 40 inches with a girth at the base of 16 to 17, and the horns have been obtained 48 inches in length and 20 in girth.

It is not found below 15,000 feet, and as it prefers the slopes of hills to the open valleys, and in its pursuit it would have been necessary to go out of our way and climb the hills, we never attempted to shoot them. Meat, not sport and trophies, was what we wanted, and antelope were much more easily got. It is found in Ladakh, where it has been known to cross with *Ovis vignei*, and we saw its horns lying about as far east as the 88th degree of longitude. The probabilities are that it is to be found still farther east. Shady stony slopes, where it is impossible to approach silently, are its favourite resting-places, and this considerably militates against the sportsman's chance of success.

The fact that sportsmen every year shoot some in Ladakh, where they have never been otherwise than scarce, points to their numbers being augmented by immigrants from across the frontier.

The *Ovis vignei* or Shapoo is found in Ladakh and Astor, and, according to Mr. Dalgleish, in Northern Tibet, but in our route across the Chang, after leaving British territory, we never saw any, nor even their horns lying about. The general elevation of the country is higher than that of the places they are found in in Ladakh, which probably accounts for their absence. They are only a climatic variety of the Oorial or Salt Range sheep, though their horns run probably a shade larger. The maximum recorded is length 37·75, girth 11·5. This species breeds freely with tame sheep, and, as has been mentioned, has been known to do so with *Ovis ammon*.

Ovis nahura.—The Burhel or Napoo is a link between the sheep and the goat tribe. It is widely distributed, and in places exceedingly common, but does not descend below 10,000 feet. It is found in Ladakh, Baltistan, and the northern slopes of the Himalayas, west of the Yarkand road, and we saw some in the country between Chiamdo and Garthok, and occasionally during our march across the Chang. It affects stony broken ground, and, although when on open ground it is a very conspicuous animal owing to the black marking on the face, chest, and legs that the males possess, amongst the strong lights and shades that are so characteristic of Tibet it is extremely hard to distinguish on the ground it prefers to rest on. Its flesh is excellent, particularly towards the end of the summer, when it is in good condition.

The largest horns recorded are length 32·1, girth 13 inches.

Cervus thoroldi or *Shoa-u-Chu.*—This grand stag, procured for the first time on this expedition when it was shot by Dr. Thorold, is found in Eastern Tibet from the neighbourhood of Tsuk Sun Dong Gong to Garthok, but does not appear to be numerous anywhere. It is found in the scrub jungle just above the forest line at elevations of about 14,000 feet. The herd out of which Dr. Thorold got two, consisted of six, all males. According to the natives they wander about a great deal, being found in different parts of country according to the time of year. If those same natives had assisted us with information, we should no doubt have succeeded in getting several; but they absolutely refused to tell us anything, or else wilfully deceived us. Under these circumstances it is apparent that in a strange country, getting an animal, whose habits one is unacquainted with, is almost entirely a matter of luck.

At present this stag's proper place amongst the Cervidæ is being discussed, and it is too early to say anything as regards its resemblances to and differences from other and better-known members of the tribe.

Dimensions :—

Length from nose to tail measured along the curve of neck	70	in.
Length of tail	4	"
Height at shoulder	48	"
Horns measured along curve	36	"
" " in a straight line	31	"
Distance from tip to tip	31½	"
Circumference of horn at base	6	"

The Tibetan wolf (*Canis laniger*) is found almost all over Tibet and the adjoining countries to the west. It is of a pale grayish colour with fine soft underwool, and the long hairs light brown tipped with black. Whether it differs from the European wolf, *Canis lupus*, or not seems to be a matter open to discussion. Its paler colour and more woolly fur appear to be the principal differences, and these may only be owing to climatic causes. In habits, however, they differ considerably. The Asiatic variety appears never to go in packs, the largest number I have seen together, and that was in the Pamirs, where they are very numerous, is six. Ordinarily they are seen in pairs or one alone. I have never heard of one attacking man, though no doubt, like the Indian wolf, it would not hesitate to take children if opportunity offered.

It is exceedingly wary, and though often seen—and we had several sheep and donkeys killed in the night by wolves, and they were often prowling around the camp—they seemed to know intuitively the range of an express rifle.

Cyon rutilans, or the wild dog, I have seen in Ladakh, but never in Tibet proper, but Hodgson obtained it from Eastern Tibet.

Ursus pruinosus.—This bear, like Dr. Thorold's stag, was obtained for the first time on this expedition, being shot in lat. 31° 58′, long. 93° 38′, at an elevation of 14,600 feet, which in that region is above the forest line, on the 30th November. Its colour is a dingy black with a broad white band round its neck, and the white from the band on its back gradually merges into the black of the under parts, thus giving it a gray appearance. It lacks intelligence more than any of the genus Ursus I have met with, none of which are particularly wary. The natives are very frightened of them, and tell stories about their attacking and mauling people, similar to the tales told of the Himalayan black bear. Our not seeing any more was probably owing to our being in the country they inhabit so late in the season when they were hibernating.

Dimensions :—

Length (total) . . .	60 in.
,, of head . . .	11 ,,
Height at shoulder . .	24 ,,

Lepus hispidus.—The upland hare is common in places and widely distributed. It affects stony ground, where it shelters amongst the rocks. As a supplement to our usual menu of antelope they did good service; had we had abundance of cartridges there would have been no difficulty in many places in shooting sufficient to feed the whole camp. In front they are of a rufescent colour with a darkish tinge on the back, and rump ashy gray. They are about the size of an English rabbit.

The Musk-Deer (*Moschus moschiferus* or *kastura*) is found throughout the Himalayas, as far west as Gilgit in Western China, and as far north as Siberia, wherever suitable country, at an elevation of about 8000 feet or more, and with brushwood or forest, is met with. The canine teeth, which sometimes measure as much as two to three inches in length, are a very conspicuous feature of this animal, which is hornless. The musk of commerce, for which it is much hunted, is the product of the male only, and is contained in a pod which holds about an ounce. The Tibetans are adepts at adulterating the musk and then closing up the pod in such a manner as to make it difficult for the uninitiated to find that it has ever been opened.

It is a solitary animal, rarely more than two being seen together, and oftener one alone.

The hair is of a peculiar kind, being long, rough, and very brittle, though undoubtedly a grand protection against cold.

The Chang is very deficient in game birds, the most widely distributed of the few that there are is the sand-grouse (*Syrrhaptes tibetanus*), a bird closely allied to, but larger than, Pallas' sand-grouse, which has recently migrated into Europe, though the probabilities of its remaining there are very doubtful.

The Tibetan sand-grouse, like all the tribe, is excellent eating, and when cartridges are scarce is a model bird to meet with, not being at all shy, and if spotted on the ground no difficulty is found in approaching within easy range. Before taking to the wing they waddle along on their ridiculously short legs for a short distance, and several can generally be got in a line before firing. We found them nesting in July, and on any one approaching their nests, pretending to be disabled, they slowly fluttered off. Once they really take to the wing they fly very strongly. About 16,000 or 17,000 feet is the elevation at which they are ordinarily seen.

SYRRHAPTES TIBETANUS.—The Tibetan sand-grouse was discovered about the year 1850, when examples were sent from Tibet to Mr. Gould by Lord Gifford, the elder brother of the late Marquis of Tweeddale. In its habits it closely resembles the European species of sand-grouse, especially in its plover-like mode of trying to decoy intruders away from its nest by feigning lameness, and pretending to be unable to fly. Dr. Thorold says that it remains on this high plateau all the year round.

H. S.

In Eastern Tibet four species of pheasant were procured. The first of these is *Crossoptilon tibetanum*

(Tibetan *shagga*, see page 178), a very large handsome bird almost entirely white, with the exception of the long feathers of the tail, which are black. They go about in flocks of about thirty, and their colour and size make them extremely conspicuous on a hill-side. Of all game birds I have ever met, they are the hardest to kill. The way we knocked feathers out of them without bringing them to book was very trying, more especially as our stock of cartridges was not large.

They were most plentiful in the neighbourhood of Riuchi.

CROSSOPTILON TIBETANUM.—Bonvalôt's Eared Pheasant was discovered in Eastern Tibet by Monsieur Bonvalôt and Prince Henri d'Orleans, during their adventurous journey in 1890 from Lob Nor to Ta-chen-lu.

A dozen or more examples are now in the museum of the Jardin des Plantes in Paris, and a fine cock and hen were brought from the same district by Captain Bower and Dr. Thorold. The latter are now in my collection and are the types of the species which was described in 1892. (Seebohm, *Bulletin of the British Ornithologists' Club*, I. page xvii.)

The examples in the Paris Museum are regarded by Monsieur Oustalêt as varieties of *Crossoptilon tibetanum*, but after careful examination of the fine series of that species brought by l'Abbé David from Moupin, and an equally fine series brought by Mr. Pratt from the mountains west of Ta-chen-lu, I am unable to agree with him in this determination. The two species appear to be perfectly distinct, and there is no example known about which there can be any doubt as to the species to which it belongs. The evidence that they interbreed where their respective areas of distribution coalesce is not in any way conclusive, and if it could be proved that they do so, the fact could not be accepted as proof that they were specifically identical, inasmuch as most of the accepted species of pheasants cross freely whenever they have a chance of doing so.

On coming down from the Chang, the great plateau of Central Tibet, across which Captain Bower and his companions travelled for many months without descending below 15,000 feet, as soon as the juniper region was reached at about 13,500 feet, the eared pheasants were seen and continued to be met with in small flocks down to about 9000 feet. The berries of this shrub (*Juniperus excelsa*) appear to be their favourite food, but sometimes they come down to feed in the cultivated fields outside the villages. They are also very fond of a sweet root or ground-nut largely eaten by the Tibetans. Their cry is a sort of whirring sound, varied at intervals by a short cluck. When disturbed on a hill-side they fly along and settle again instead of shooting down to the bottom as most of the Himalayan pheasants do. They perch freely on trees, and are plentiful in Eastern Tibet up to the limit of forest growth. The Tibetan name is Shagga. They are very hard to kill, and generally escape from shot unless a pellet passes through the head.

CROSSOPTILON LEUCURUM (see page 182).—Hodgson's Eared Pheasant was discovered about the year 1830, when a single example was brought to Nepal by the Nepalese envoys to Pekin on their return journey.

This example remained unique until l'Abbé David rediscovered this fine species in the mountains near Moupin in Western China. It remained a very rare bird in collections until Mr. Pratt found it in great abundance at Mousimien in the mountains to the west of Ta-chen-lu in 1890.

Both Monsieur Bonvalôt and Captain Bower found it in small flocks in Eastern Tibet in the company of its close ally, Bonvalôt's Eared Pheasant, and neither of the travellers regarded the two forms as distinct species. H. S.

Phasianus elegans (see page 244) we only found at one place, that was amongst the scrub in the river bed at Ta-chen-lu. It is quite a different style of bird from the other three, and much resembles the pheasants of England and Turkistan. They are fairly numerous, and we might have had excellent sport with them had we not run out of cartridges.

PHASIANUS ELEGANS.—Anderson's Pheasant was discovered by Dr. Anderson at Momien in Western Yunan, and received the manuscript name of *Phasianus sladeni* (Anderson, *Proc. Zool. Soc.*, 1871, page 214), but before any description was published, two living examples were deposited in the Zoological Gardens in London, which had been sent by the Chinese collectors of Mr. I. J. Stone from the slopes of the Yung-ling Mountains in Eastern Tibet west of Ta-chen-lu. The latter were described as *Phasianus elegans* (Elliot, *Ann. Nat. Hist.*, series 4, vi. page 312).

Both these discoveries had, however, been forestalled more than thirty years ago. There is a mounted example in the gallery of the British Museum which was presented to the National Collection by the late Mr. J. R. Reeves. On the stand a memorandum is written, stating that this example was brought alive from China and was deposited in the Zoological Gardens in London, where it died in the year 1839. I have not been able to discover that this example ever received a name. H. S.

Ithaginis geoffroyi (Tibetan *Tsiri*).—The Blood Pheasant (see page 199) is found at elevations of about 10,000 feet, and affects thick cover. Its colour is a peculiar mixture of gray, pale green, and pink, giving it altogether the appearance of being artificially dyed. It has a smaller beak than most of the pheasant tribe, and a tuft on its head completes its appearance as the least gamey-looking of all game birds I know. In places they are very numerous, but one can go through considerable stretches of apparently suitable country without seeing any. Several were shot by officers during the late Sikkim expedition.

ITHAGINIS GEOFFROYI.—The Chauveau's Blood Pheasant was discovered about five-and-twenty years ago by Père Chauveau, a French missionary, who found it on the mountains above Ta-chen-lu, and sent examples to Paris through the French Consul to Hankau (Sclater, *Ibis*, 1870, page 297).

Captain Bower found that it does not range so high as the eared pheasant, and generally affects thicker cover. It is not so strong on the wing, nor does it as readily take to flight, and when up it flies to the nearest tree, where it sits in an absurdly tame manner. It is not so gregarious as the eared pheasant. Occasionally several were found together in the same little bit of jungle, but when disturbed they did not stick together like a herd of sheep as the eared pheasants do. H. S.

Tetraophasis szechenyii (Tibetan *Koonon*, see page 235) much resembles a large grouse, but has a conspicuous white bar across the tail. It is a much more sporting bird than the Tsiri, and takes boldly to the wing when disturbed. The elevation at which they are found is very similar to the elevation at which the other two are found, but it is fonder of the jungle than the Shagga, though I have found all these three birds on the same ground. They all perch on trees.

TETRAOPHASIS SZECHENYII.—Szechenyi's Snow Partridge was discovered during the unsuccessful expedition to Tibet under Count Bela Szechenyi, and was described as coming from East Tibet (Madarasz, *Zeitschrift für die Gesammte Ornithologie*, 1885, page 50), but the locality was afterwards corrected to Central Tibet (Madarasz, *Ibis*, 1886, page 145). The description is accompanied by a plate which represents a bird rather paler in colour than those procured by Captain Bower and Dr. Thorold.

Very shortly after its discovery it was redescribed under the name of *Tetraophasis desgodinsi* (Oustalet, *Le Naturaliste*, 1886, page 276) from examples sent by l'Abbé Desgodins from Yerkalo at the extreme north point of the province of Yunan, about a degree nearly due south of Bathang. These examples agree with others obtained by Monsieur Bonvalôt and Prince Henri d'Orleans, and with those obtained by Captain Bower and Dr. Thorold in Eastern Tibet.

Captain Bower further remarks that its range extends higher than that of the Blood Pheasant, sometimes above the limit of forest growth, but not as high as that of the Eared Pheasant.

It is a fairly good flyer, frequenting the jungle and scrub, but roosting in trees. Occasionally five or six are found together, but no large flocks were observed. H. S.

TETRAOGALLUS HIMALAYENSIS.—The Himalayan Snow Partridge was discovered as long ago as 1842 in the Himalaya Mountains, and has since been found also to inhabit S.W. Siberia.

Captain Bower found it to be a common resident species on the high central plateau of Tibet, where it is known under the native name of *ram chukar*. H. S.

TETRASTES SEVERTZOVI.—Prjevalski's Hazel Grouse was discovered in 1872 in the mountain forests of Kansu, whence many examples were brought by General Prjevalski to St. Petersburg. It was procured by Captain Bower and his companions in Eastern Tibet, but neither of these travellers has described its habits. H. S.

TETRASTES SEVERTZOVI.

PERDIX SIFANICA (see page 130).—Prjevalski's Partridge was discovered in the Nan Shan Mountains, between Koko Nor and the western extremity of the Great Wall of China, by General Prjevalski (Rowley's *Ornithological Miscellany*, ii. page 423). It was found in Eastern Tibet both by Monsieur Bonvalôt and Captain Bower. H. S.

The Coolen (*Grus cinerea*) of Europeans in India, Koon of the Punjab, and Cha toon toon of Tibet, is the well-known crane of Europe. Its colour is an ashy gray with a black forehead, chin, throat, foreneck, and tail.

We saw them at camp No. 54 on 6th October, each pair of old birds accompanied by a pair of young ones which, though nearly as big as the parent birds, were gray all over. In India they go about in large flocks and commit great depredations amongst the crops. They are excellent eating.

The Bar-headed Goose (*Anser indicus*) is a bird that visits India in great numbers in the cold weather. Taking Upper India (including Sind), Hume says, "this species enormously outnumbers all the other species of geese put together." It breeds on the Chang, and in August we found the young nearly full grown but unable to fly, on pools of fresh water. We did not, however, see nearly enough to warrant the assertion that the region we were in was the regular nesting-place of the enormous numbers that visit India in the cold weather—the presumption is that the great mass of them go farther north. The lakes of Tibet, being nearly all intensely salt, are unsuitable for either bird or fish life, and even on the fresh-water pools there was a great absence of weeds or other suitable food. Brahminy ducks, which we saw, may occasionally breed, but even they, as I have myself observed, are at least fifty times as numerous in summer on the river and swamps between Kashgar and Lob Nor in Chinese Turkistan. No other ducks breed in Tibet, so far as I have seen; snipe may occasionally do so where there are springs of fresh water and a little marshy ground.

ANSER INDICUS.—The Bar- or Barred-headed Goose was known to be an inhabitant of Tibet in Latham's time, one hundred years ago.

In the autumn, immense flights were seen winging their way towards India, where they winter. H. S.

Six species of butterfly were found at elevations varying from 15,500 to 17,600, viz.—

Æneis pumulus	Pieris chloridice
Vanessa ladakensis	Parnassius acco
Synchloë butleri	„ jacquemontii

These were collected by Dr. Thorold, and so far as we know included every butterfly seen by us in Tibet. That any at all were found on these cold wind-swept plains was a matter of surprise to me.

Minimum Temperature Chart. Observations by Dr. Thorold. I.M.S.

June 1891.				July 1891.				August 1891.			
Date.	Place and Altitude.		Degree F.	Date.	Place and Altitude.		Degree F.	Date.	Place and Altitude.		Degree F.
		Feet.				Feet.				Feet.	
1				1	Camp	16,975	+23°	1	Camp XX	17,082	+30°
2				2	Camp under Lanak	17,315	+24°	2	Do. ,,	17,082	+28°
3				3	Shum (Tibet)	17,600	+19°	3	Do. ,,	17,082	+24°
4				4	Tobomarpo Lanak	17,550	+17°	4	Do. XXI	16,482	+26°
5				5	Kalung ,,	17,680	+18°	5	Do. XXII	16,282	+31°
6				6	Papuk ,,	17,694	+19°	6	Do. ,,	16,282	+34°
7				7	Do. ,,	17,694	+18°	7	Do. XXIII	16,082	+27°
8				8	Camp I	17,650	+20°	8	Do. ,,	16,082	+31°
9				9	Do. II	17,850	+18°	9	Do. XXIV	15,799	+31°
10				10	Do. III	17,935	+20°	10	Do. XXV	15,999	+35°
11				11	Do. IV	17,990	+23°	11	Do. XXVI	16,074	+34°
12				12	Do. V	18,315	+22°	12	Do. XXVII	17,351	+28°
13				13	Do. VI	17,815	+30°	13	Do. XXVIII	16,526	+29°
14				14	Do. ,,	17,815	+24°	14	Do. XXIX	16,551	+28°
15				15	Do. VII	16,189	+24°	15	Do. XXX	16,907	+28°
16				16	Do. VIII	16,500	+26°	16	Do. XXXI	16,907	+21°
17				17	Do. IX	16,899	+30°	17	Do. XXXII	16,647	+21°
18				18	Do. X	16,874	+29°	18	Do. XXXIII	16,747	+19°
19				19	Do. XI	17,274	+29°	19	Do. XXXIV	16,767	+23°
20				20	Do. XII	17,176	+29°	20	Do. XXXV	16,167	+26°
21	Zingral	15,800	+18°	21	Arurapka Camp XIII	17,276	+27°	21	Do. XXXVI	15,967	+23°
22	Durga	13,000	+34°	22	Domra ,, XIV	17,701	+25°	22	Do. XXXVII	15,547	+27°
23	Tankse	13,000	+33°	28	Camp XV	17,501	+27°	28	Do. XXXVIII	15,353	+29°
24	Do.	13,000	+33°	24	Do. XVI	17,501	+29°	24	Do. ,,	15,353	+30°
25	Chakka Talao	13,600	+33°	25	Do. XVII	17,600	+29°	25	Do. XXXIX	15,146	+31°
26	Pobrang	14,500	+29°	26	Do. ,,	17,600	+22°	26	Do. XL	15,171	+29°
27	Camp below Marsa-mik La	16,600	+18°	27	Do. XVIII	16,837	+26°	27	Do. XLI	15,346	+27°
28	Rundi Gainle	16,800	+27°	28	Do. XIX	16,762	+29°	28	Do. XLII	14,796	+24°
29	Pamzal	15,475	+22°	29	Do. XX	17,082	+28°	29	Do. XLIII	14,621	+31°
30	Kyam	16,000	+28°	30	Do. ,,	17,082	+26°	30	Do. XLIV	14,796	+32°
				31	Do. ,,	17,082	+29°	31	Do. XLV	15,621	+31°

Minimum Temperature Chart (continued).

September 1891.				October 1891.			
Date.	Place and Altitude.		Degree F.	Date.	Place and Altitude.		Degree F.
		Feet.				Feet.	
1	Camp XLVI	15,348	+29°	1	Camp LI	15,560	+21°
2	Do. XLVII	15,773	+29°	2	Do. ,,	15,560	+20°
3	Do. XLVIII	16,148	+21°	3	Do. ,,	15,560	+19°
4	Do. ,,	16,148	+27°	4	Kammuk Camp LII	15,560	+20°
5	Do. XLIX	15,523	+32°	5	Toraz do. LIII	15,660	+19°
6	Do. L	15,423	+31°	6	Churro do. LIV	15,210	+17°
7	Do. LI	15,560	+33°	7	Do. do. LV	15,876	+18°
8	Gagalinchin	15,560	+35°	8	Tobrak do. LVI	16,400	+16°
9	Do.	15,560	+35°	9	Lumakans do. LVII	15,348	+18°
10	Do.	15,560	+36°	10	Do. do. ,,	15,348	+16°
11	Do.	15,560	+32°	11	Do. do. ,,	15,348	+15°
12	Do.	15,560	+35°	12	Urnúi do. LVIII	15,500	+15°
13	Do.	15,560	+31°	13	Mongapeshor Camp LIX	15,500	+16°
14	Do.	15,560	+29°	14	Hormo Suchuk do. LX	15,463	+17°
15	Do.	15,560	+24°	15	Mangusa do. LXI	15,538	+18°
16	Do.	15,560	+23°	16	Do. do. ,,	15,538	+10°
17	Do.	15,560	+24°	17	Tugla Gispo do. LXII	16,238	+ 8°
18	Do.	15,560	+20°	18	Camp LXIII	16,668	+ 7°
19	Do.	15,560	+20°	19	Do. LXIV	16,363	+ 5°
20	Do.	15,560	+19°	20	Do. LXV	15,760	+ 3°
21	Do.	15,560	+21°	21	Do. ,,	15,760	+ 4°
22	Do.	15,560	+22°	22	Do. LXVI	16,263	+ 8°
23	Do.	15,560	+19°	23	Do. LXVII	16,563	+ 3°
24	Do.	15,560	+20°	24	Do. LXVIII	15,863	+ 8°
25	Do.	15,560	+21°	25	Do. LXIX	16,663	+ 4°
26	Do.	15,560	+30°	26	Do. LXX	16,538	+ 2°
27	Do.	15,560	+28°	27	Do. LXXI	16,838	− 4°
28	Do.	15,560	+24°	28	Do. ,,	16,838	−11°
29	Do.	15,560	+26°	29	Do. ,,	16,838	−14°
30	Do.	15,560	+26°	30	Do. LXXII	16,763	−12°
				31	Do. LXXIII	16,263	−15°

Minimum Temperature Chart (concluded).

NOVEMBER 1891.

Date.	Place and Altitude.		Feet.	Degree F.
1	Camp	LXXIV	16,463	– 10°
2	Do.	LXXV	16,363	– 15°
3	Do.	LXXVI	16,113	– 15°
4	Do.	LXXVII	16,238	– 8°
5	Do.	LXXVIII	16,148	– 10°
6	Do.	LXXIX	16,139	– 1°
7	Do.	LXXX	15,689	– 11°
8	Do.	LXXXI	15,439	– 13°
9	Do.	"	15,439	– 14°
10	Do.	LXXXII	15,194	– 3°
11	Do.	LXXXIII	15,389	– 6°
12	Do.	LXXXIV	15,469	+ 13°
13	Do.	LXXXV	15,694	+ 2°
14	Do.	LXXXVI	15,439	0°
15	Do.	LXXXVII	14,890	– 7°
16	Do.	"	14,890	– 8°
17	Do.	LXXXVIII	14,740	– 11°
18	Do.	LXXXIX Atak Thomar	14,925	+ 17°
19	Do.	XC do.	14,925	+ 20°
20	Do.	XCI	14,900	*
21	Do.	XCII	14,525	+ 3°
22	Do.	XCIII	14,325	– 11°
23	Do.	XCIV	14,200	– 4°
24	Do.	XCV	14,025	– 3°
25	Do.	XCVI	14,025	+ 11°
26	Do.	XCVII	14,450	+ 14°
27	Do.	XCVIII	14,850	+ 4°
28	Do.	XCIX	14,950	+ 2°
29	Do.	"	14,950	+ 1°
30	Do.	C	14,650	+ 7°

DECEMBER 1891.

Date.	Place and Altitude.		Feet.	Degree F.
1	Camp	CI Tsuk Sun Dong Gong	13,210	+ 13°
2	Do.	CII	13,425	+ 9°
3	Do.	CIII	13,400	+ 7°
4	Do.	CIV	13,825	+ 13°
5	Do.	CV	14,060	+ 14°
6	Do.	"	14,060	+ 8°
7	Do.	CVI	13,325	+ 3°
8	Richando	CVII	13,225	+ 1°
9	Camp	CVIII Pata Samdo	13,325	+ 1°
10	Do.	"	13,325	+ 1°
11	Do.	CIX	14,100	+ 4°
12	Do.	CX Sari Samdu	12,063	*

* Thermometer broke.

INDEX

THE END